Real Estate Simplified: Unlocking Lasting & Total Success

WENDY LEE

ISBN: 978-1-938495-01-4

DEDICATION

This book is dedicated to my parents. It is their work ethic and belief system that is engrained in my passion, purpose and mission to be all that I can be for my clients and partners.

Working at the family business in the restaurant industry ever since the tender age of 8, I have always learned the value of the hard earned dollar. As a result, I have never rented an apartment, or leased a car. I have always also said if you have to ask how much it is, then you can't afford it. I have always had more of a penny wise school of thought, so the 1st time I moved out of Mom and Dad's house was when I moved into my own condo. Over the last decade, I have purchased several pieces of property and even assisted immediate family to purchase investment property.

My wish for you reading this book, that I help you as well in assisting you with attaining your real estate investing goals. It is my pleasure to sit down with you to discuss your real estate objectives, and offer you an action plan based on your goals, time frame to achieve those goals.

CONTENTS

FOREWORD

To buy or not to buy real estate?

Actually, if you chose to not buy real estate, then you are not allowing yourself to LIVE OUT LOUD…

One of the cornerstones of creating generational wealth would be to invest in real estate. Real estate is an asset while flat screen televisions, fancy cars, luxury purses are not good investments. Do these kinds of purchases make you money like real estate would? Winning the approval of your friends, do not pay the bills. So stop this madness!! It is a great time to buy real estate.

As the current market conditions are getting better and better, there is no time but the present to buy. Consumer confidence has been building over the last three years since the rebound of the market. In fact, you should have been sweeping up a ton of cheap real estate 10 years ago when we first saw signs of the economic downturn overall. If you have people who are telling you not to buy, let me ask you a question. Who is the one that has wealth and investments to show for? Those who told you not to buy or those who have been buying since the economy crashed.

"Don't wait to buy real estate. Buy real estate and wait." -- Will Rogers

The strategy to build wealth is to buy low, sell high. You can buy locally or in another state as long as you have a team that you can truly count on to oversee the day to day operation of the acquired real investments. As long as you have a winning team to guide you along the way, then you will be fine.

If you are thinking of buying real estate to invest in, then you should consider Wendy Lee's book, RESULTS - Real Estate Simplified: Unlocked Lasting & Total Success, Keys to a Happy, Healthy Home. She and a team of expert real estate professionals have collaborated to bring you this great book that will give a better appreciation of every step of the sales transaction from start to finish.

Wendy's purpose was to create a book that will involve all of her real estate partners that would be able to provide you a detailed vantage point of what is needed in that part of the real estate transaction, so you can fully understand the process and how each partner's part in the process play in ensuring your interests are being addressed and secured by that business partner.

It starts off with a chapter from a well-known financial and wealth coach. She presents to you her WEALTHY Blueprint which helps create a solid framework to assist the perspective buyer to buy real estate and how to follow through the system so that one can achieve their financial goals.

This book also discusses on how credit affects your ability to buy property. Cracking the Credit Code Steps helps re-establishing your credit.

It discusses the mechanics and tools used in doing search to identify the ideal piece of real estate to start your investment portfolio.

This book then takes you through other major milestones during the sales transaction. It offers you real estate home inspector key notes and a checklist of items that the inspector goes over during a formal property inspection.

A real estate attorney discusses the steps they follow for their clients to protect their interests while legally protecting them from any issues that may arise during the attorney review process.

This book even offers a chapter that discusses on how to maintain a happy, healthy home by following a few Feng Shui practices to secure positive energy flow in your home.

Lastly, it offers the five pitfalls of wealth you must be aware of and avoid to ensure keeping more wealth and creating more wealth.

Throughout all my years of creating wealth and helping build wealth for others and turning them into millionaires, real estate has played a major role. Wendy Lee simplifies the process and makes buying and selling real estate a smooth transaction.

Loral Langemeier
The Millionaire Maker
Five Time New York Times Bestselling Author

INTRODUCTION

Humans have always had a basic need for shelter.

And shelter has evolved today to what we call "home." We all want a place to call home. Home is our personal sanctuary. A place where we could safely be ourselves and relax.

Home vs House. Home has personal emotional connection. House has a practical and utilitarian perspective.

Regardless of the size of the home or dwelling, the space we call home has a direct influence in our lives. Our homes are a mirror of our lives.

Finding and purchasing a home is no easy task. With the help of a qualified Real Estate Agent, the process can become manageable.

We've been brought together, to give you simple steps and a practical outlook so you can have a piece of that pie: The Dream of owning your home and making it yours.

WHY IS OWNING A HOME SO IMPORTANT?

There is a certain amount of realization and joy that comes with making a statement such as:

"We just bought our first home," or "I just purchased my first apartment."

For me, it's always been important to own a home. Having a place of my own meant a kind freedom I'd never had before. It was a chance to put my special mark into a place that had more than four walls.

At first, the idea of owning a home gave me something to work towards. The goal to save for a down payment.

Realizing that there are many neighborhoods out there, made us really think about where to purchase, because having a permanent place to live meant putting our roots down.

Choosing a neighborhood meant that we found a place where we belong. This is the community we enjoy living in now and for the next 20 years raising our children.

We've been told growing up that owning your own place is a great investment. My family was proud of us for making the big step. It gave our children a community that could nurture and help them grow. Having great schools and access to a network of extracurricular activities was very important.

So, with our family's support and the keys to our own place, we embarked on a journey of belonging.

If you are like the majority of us, you cannot wait to clean your new place, paint it, maybe gut it, make some changes and move-in.

A new homeowner has no shortage of ideas to make the new place truly feel "yours." We were no different; we made changes inside and outside.

Putting our signature, our "stamp" in this new place was an exciting project.

After all, our new home had become our personal space and an extension of who we are.

The Benefits of making your Home "yours"

The benefits are many. Here are some general ones to get started:

- Makes you feel safe
- Be comfortable to be yourself

- A place where you could be Creative
- Explore beyond boundaries
- Set new goals and aspirations
- Deepen your connection with others • Try new hobbies
- Helps you set the next phase of your life • Work with nature
- Find meaning in your life
- Have a place for inner balance

Are you ready?

Now is your turn. In the section of the book, write down your reasons for buying a home. Write them all, you'd be surprised where they lead you.

CHAPTER 1: THE WEALTH SYSTEM

By Melanie Jane Nicolas

INTRODUCTION

As the CEO and Founder of World of Wealth Group and Kids Wealth International Club, and a "mompreneur" with four kids, I found that the secret to a solid foundation for your pathway to financial success is utilizing a tool called the WEALTH System. This section is designed for you to understand the concept of the WEALTH System so that you can begin to implement the system with success. This will also create great habits regarding money savings and management.

The WEALTH System is a system in which all of your money is allocated into six distinct categories, aka the six jobs of money, so that you always have money for all your needs. The six jobs are Wealth, Education, Accumulation, Living, Tithe, and Happy. You can utilize separate bank accounts, envelopes, or jars to do this. To illustrate this system, I will utilize jars as an example.

As a child, you probably received money through allowances and gifts and spend it. The majority of parents do not teach their kids how to spend their money; much less teach their kids how money works. There are no standards as to how their child should spend the money. I know…because these were my parents. In addition, I would like to suggest that your money has more of a purpose than just spending. In a recent survey, three out of four Americans live paycheck to paycheck. At the end of the month, all the money is spent, and there is nothing left over to save or invest. This has caused Americans to increasingly turn to their credit cards, resulting in credit card debt becoming a big problem in America. By reading this section, along with going through a financial education camp like KWIC World of Wealth Camp and Your

WEALTHY Business Blueprint, you will not only gain the six fundamental knowledge of how to allocate your money, but the skills to becoming financially successful. So have fun with this! You are on your way to becoming a financially responsible individual for yourself, your family, and generations to come.

WEALTH JAR

"The true value of a human being is determined primarily by the measure and the sense in which he has attained to liberation from the self." -Albert Einstein

One of the most important habits that wealthy people have is "paying yourself first." However, because most individuals don't understand this concept, we naturally do the exact opposite by paying everyone else first, leaving no money to invest in assets that grow over time. Assets are divided into two categories: cash flow assets and appreciating assets. The three main investments you can invest in are stocks, businesses, and real estate. When you invest at an early age, you will find that the key to financial freedom is growing your assets. Some ways you can invest are investing in stocks, bonds, mutual funds, coins, and cash accumulating life insurance policies. You can also use your money in your own business. Lastly, you can invest your money in real estate properties, growing your equity, and profiting when you sell your home and it is worth more than when you purchased it. The key to the Wealth Jar is that you never take out the money unless it makes you money.

When my oldest daughter was five years old, we had a fundraiser for our church. We made desserts called halo-halo and sold them for $5. I told my daughter that I would give her $2 for every halo-halo she makes, and I would keep $1 for the ingredients and give $2 to our church. She then turned to me and asked, "Can I just have my friend Francis make them, and I can give him $1?" I was amazed that she understood the concept of leveraging people's time, a skill that entrepreneurs have. This is when I realized that kids are creative entrepreneurs.

We dreamt as kids to become entrepreneurs. There are many stories of kids who started their own businesses, which grew into functioning and profitable enterprises. Chances are, you still have entrepreneurship in you. You are fully capable of using your creative mind to invest your money in your Wealth Jar. All you need to do is start.

Allocate 10% of your money into your Wealth Jar.

Take a moment and list 12 ways you can invest, one for each month.

EDUCATION JAR

"If you wish to achieve worthwhile things in your personal and career life, you must become a worthwhile person in your own self-development." -Brian Tracy

Every parent wants their child to be educated. Education is important because what a child learns is the foundation of his life. Think about it: a child spends all of his childhood in school. This is where he practically learns all the basic fundamentals of life. But why is it that most adults won't spend half the money to invest in themselves by learning things not taught in school? Could it be because children got used to believing parents should put them through school and so education stops after college when they get a "good and secure" job? Not only is college education important, but personal development as well. When you develop the habit of putting money aside in your Education Jar, you learn that education is crucial to your continuous growth. To instill in yourself that life is a continuous education process is priceless. According to Tony Robbins, "If you are not growing, you are dying." Personal development can expose you to the importance of creative thinking, goal-setting, and problem solving. Being exposed to our KWIC Mini-Camps and Your WEALTHY Business Blueprint Program or other personal development programs can not only give you more tools, but also create everlasting relationships with other entrepreneurs. Most adults do not discover personal development until they are much older. Exposing yourself to this other form of education is crucial. Other things you can use your money in the Education Jar for are books, real estate seminars and even Feng Shui.

Allocate 10% of your money into your Education Jar.

Take a moment and list 12 ways you can start educating yourself.

ACCUMULATION JAR

"Dare to dream of your great success. Become intimate with those things which deeply motivate you and regularly work toward the realization of that mission." -Mary Anne Radmacher

Do you remember as a child often drawing about what could be? Funny, but as adults we forget to dream because of all the negativity we encounter throughout our lives. This next jar is the Savings Jar. The Savings Jar has two functions. Primarily, it is for emergency money. An example of this is your car breaking down unexpectedly and you need funds to repair it. Secondarily, the Savings Jar is for long-term savings. This jar helps you to dream about something you want, and to also set a goal to achieve it. It could be something like saving for a new car or money for a family vacation. Whatever it is, allow yourself to dream big. When you set out a dream, you naturally learn how to set goals. The skill of goal setting is an important factor to succeed in life. You get what you set out to do and think of most.

Allocate 10% of your money into your Savings Jar: 5% for emergency money and 5% for a long-term goal purchase.

Take a moment and list six emergency needs you may need to save up for.

List six larger purchases you want to achieve, and then choose and circle the one you will save up for first.

Write a statement in achieving this number one goal of yours. It should be clear, specific, and measurable.

LIVING JAR

"Learn to live with less. Learn to shun envy. Appreciate what you have. If you have less, you will appreciate what you have more." - Anonymous

Your Living Jar is for living expenses. These are things such as your mortgage, utilities, car expenses, food, and major insurance policies. It is very important to track your living expenses. It is one of the most important skills in money management. I am a firm believer that kids should be taught this skill at an early age. Now you are probably thinking, my kid doesn't make enough money to pay for his living expenses. To make this simple, ask your child to contribute 50% or their allowances to the basic needs of the family, such as food, clothing, utilities, car, etc. This will really teach them to become responsible, and they will build confidence in managing their own money.

Allocate 50% of your money into your Living Jar.

Take a moment and list all your living expenses. Add up all your expenses and determine whether you are living on 50% of your income. If not, determine which expenses are things you want and are really not needs. If you are living on 50% of your income, you are in a great position in laying your financial foundation to reach financial freedom.

TITHE JAR

"No act of kindness, however small, is ever wasted." -Aesop

Giving and tithing to the community not only allows you to be aware of your blessings, but it also builds character. For kids, giving teaches them to think beyond themselves and thus, they learn to be generous, compassionate people. Giving to the world can be actions such as making a tithing to the church, buying toys for a charity such as Toys For Tots and APPEAR (APPEARtoday.org), and purchasing a gift for a good friend.

When my son turned three years old, we had leftover cupcakes from his birthday party. He wanted more cupcakes than I would allow him to have. I thought this would be a great opportunity to teach him a life principle so I told him we're giving the cupcakes away to the local shelter. At first he was hesitant, but when I encouraged him that giving is a huge act of kindness, we drove over to the shelter. We walked into the shelter and had a whole tray of cupcakes. We walked around and gave one cupcake to every person in the building. Each person said, "Oh, he's so cute. Thank you so much. You just brightened up my day." You can imagine what this did for my son's self-esteem. He did not see that giving was taking away something from him, and it made him feel good to give. Ever since then, he loves taking money out of his Tithe Jar to donate or buy something for the local shelter in need.

Allocate 10% of your money into your Tithe Jar. Take a moment and list 12 ways your child can give or tithe to the community.

HAPPY JAR

"Play is the only way the highest intelligence of humankind can unfold." -Joseph Chilton Pearce

Once your money is allocated into the previously mentioned jars, it is time to play. Yay! You should spend all of your money in your Happy Jar on things and activities that make you happy. The Happy Jar is to be spent on a monthly basis, and there are no limits as to how to spend this. As a mom, I saw so many moms, including myself, giving to their kids and not to themselves. I quickly learned that I was modelling to my kids that they are not worthy or rewarding themselves. You are deserving of rewarding yourself, which many of us adults feel guilty about. Your hard earned money is a means to the rewards. For me, this includes serving myself by enjoying massages, treating myself to a good meal, and going on a retreat. Give yourself your heart's desires as the highest vibrational energy is self-love.

Allocate 10% of your money into your Happy Jar.

Take a moment and list 12 ways you can use your Happy Jar.

BUILDING THE FOUNDATION TODAY

The WEALTH System is just the beginning to your financial success. Our KWIC World of Wealth Camp http://kwickid.com/camps/minicamp/ goes into more detail regarding this system, while teaching other concepts around money in a fun, accelerated learning way. For more information on our World of Wealth Group Financial Workshops, visit http://worldofwealthgroup.com/ and schedule your WOW Financial Lifestyle Strategy Session.

In conclusion, when you allocate your money from work and gifts, it is important to have set percentages as to how that money will be used. Now that you understand that money has six different jobs, through the WEALTH System, you can now manage your money more effectively so you will always have money for everything you need. Start this WEALTH System and begin to build your financial foundation to become financially free.

MEET THE CONTRIBUTOR

One of the most exciting and sought-out speakers in North America, Melanie Jane Nicolas has committed her life to teaching children, their parents, and small business owners to utilize her proven wealth-creation systems to raise wealthy individuals and create the first financially responsible generation. Melanie Jane Nicolas is the CEO and Founder of World of Wealth Group and Kids Wealth International Club. As America's Leading Authority in Raising Wealthy Kids, she empowers children to live a healthier financial future by helping kids get rich in a fun way. She is the author of several books and is the best-selling author of *Raising Wealthy Kids: 7 Steps for Creating the First Financially Responsible Generation.* Melanie Jane's highly innovative techniques and strategies show how to raise our children to be future leaders. Renowned for her passion for and total commitment to the children, parents, and small business owners she teaches, Melanie Jane seizes every opportunity to demonstrate the power of her teachings, teachings she herself lives by with her four children each and every day. These are the same wealth principles taught to thousands of children who are living happy, healthy, and wealthy lives. Melanie Jane is now living her life purpose of being a great servant of God through her work, a wonderful mother of four, and an innovative, passionate business mentor with a special message for a large audience.

But it wasn't always this way…

Born into a middle class family in Chicago, Illinois, Melanie Jane with her brother lived with parents who taught them that getting a good education and a secure job is the secret to success. Her parents made many sacrifices, including sending her to the Philippines to be raised by an 18-year-old nanny so that they can work two jobs here in the United States without the hassle of finding a babysitter. When she was seven years old, she returned to the United States.

After spending some time with entrepreneurs during her adolescent years, Melanie Jane realized at the age of 13 that she wanted to be an entrepreneur. She had a passion for children as well, taking numerous babysitting jobs and aspired to what she thought she wanted to be, a pediatrician. Her experience growing up greatly influenced who she is today. Her mom was a nurse, working long hours, and her dad was an engineer, who later built a construction company.

With a passion to help people, Melanie Jane graduated with a Bachelor of Science in Nursing in 1998 and worked as an Operating Room Nurse at Lutheran General Hospital and Swedish Covenant Hospital, specializing in orthopedic and neurologic surgeries. With her leadership skills, she also took on the role of the charge nurse, which involves collaboratively working with surgeons and anesthesiologists to efficiently and effectively optimize the care of all the patients undergoing surgery. After working for seven years, Melanie Jane retired and bought New Beginning General Homecare Services with some partners.

While working as a registered nurse, Melanie Jane also retained her real estate license in 1999 and bought her first property at the age of 22. She worked side by side with her father who was a general contractor, where she became an expert in real estate. Since then, Melanie Jane has owned and invested in over 100 properties with a team and helped many families with their real estate needs.

Melanie Jane has two passions in life: children and entrepreneurship. She has four beautiful children. Her challenge with becoming an entrepreneur is that growing up she never had the mentors she needed to have that success mindset. She watched her parents go through the financial roller coaster ride, living in a millionaire dollar home one year, and then filing bankruptcy the next. Until one day, her dad suffered a heart attack that nearly killed him because of the stress of money. It was then when she sought out mentors in finance and business to teach her the rules of the money game and win. And because of her love for children, she founded Kids Wealth International Club, Helping Your Kids Get Rich in a Fun Way. Although it was rewarding teaching kids wealth principles such as "Pay Yourself First," and "Save Early Save Often," she quickly found that when the kids would go back home to their parents, the parents would undo all the wealth beliefs and habits because they didn't know how to support them. That's when she and her team at World of Wealth Group started educating families as well. Within a year, she grew her team of over 30 licensed associates, educating families to save, invest, retire, protect their financial foundation, and become financially free so that they can live the lifestyle of their dreams. Here, Melanie Jane continues to educate on the systems of building a profitable business and becoming an entrepreneur.

Melanie Jane is a strong believer in continuous growth and contributing to the world. Because of this, she has trained with many millionaire mentors and continues a process of unending self-education which has distinguished her as an authority in empowering young entrepreneurs as she continues to share her knowledge and expertise. With this, Melanie Jane became the pioneer leader of the Young Entrepreneur Society Mastermind Forum Chapter in Park Ridge and Naperville, Illinois where she helps other entrepreneurs discover the information that she has learned to add value into their lives. She is also very involved in her community, volunteering her time and knowledge as the Treasurer of the Naperville Safety Town Commission and teaching kids at schools through the Savvy Business Kids Program. Melanie Jane feels so blessed with an awesome life. She loves her children and thanks God for His most precious gifts every day. Because of her four children, her passion is children…to inspire and empower them with an abundant mindset so that they can make a positive impact in this world. She strives to adopt at least 100 kids from all over the world through projects such as Partners International. She also founded APPEAR™ – The Association of Proud Parents Educating About Riches so that she can educate parents around the world on how to provide their children a life of abundant wealth in values of FAITH, FAMILY, FITNESS, FINANCE,

FUN. Her foundation donated over $300K to charities serving children who are in need, such as St. Jude's Cancer Research Society and Feed My Starving Children.

CHAPTER 2:
CRACKING THE CREDIT CODE

By Joy R. Sinegar-Munoz

Credit is a constant in our lives. It can be a reminder of the wrong turns we've taken or the good choices we've made. At the end of the day, as much as we hate that, credit hangs over our heads, it can do so many positive things for us. It can create wealth, open businesses, and provide a place to live. Credit is a vital piece of our financial stability, so we must use it to advance our lives and the lies of the people we care about.

There are three separate credit agencies or bureaus (Equifax, Experian & Transunion) which collect and report information about how we use our credit. These three agencies also store and report our personal data such as addresses, date of birth, and previous employers.

Lenders, employers, and other entities from which you apply for credit; rely on the scores from either all or one of the scores presented by the credit bureaus to help determine if you are a good candidate to lend to.

WHAT DO CREDIT SCORES MEAN?

The FICO or Fair Isaac Corporation score model is derived from historical data on your credit, including your usage of revolving and installment debt. Additionally, credit scores are affected by collections, judgments, the age of bankruptcies, and foreclosures. Each range of credit score helps determine your creditworthiness:

800+ = is considered an excellent score and would be marked as a low risk borrower to a potential lender.

740-799 = a very good score and would mean that you'd likely get the best rates and terms from many lenders.

670-739 – a good credit score and you would likely receive mid-range rates and terms from a potential lender.

580-669 = this is a fair credit score and is below what all bureaus consider to be "average"

579-Lower = this is a poor score. You have a good chance of being rejected for credit.

WHERE DO WE BEGIN?

RECLAIMING YOUR CREDIT

The first step to any financial decision should involve a long, hard look at your credit report. Go to a reputable website such as www.annualcreditreport.com to request a copy of your report. Request a report from all three bureaus in order to compare all information between them. It is important that all information is reviewed for errors and discrepancies.

The most common errors are names, addresses, and places of employment. A misspelling of your name on your credit file can mean finding someone else's bad credit on your report. Also, if you are a person that shares a name with a close family member, you have to be certain that their credit does not merge onto your file.

By understanding your credit file, you'll be in a better position to make adjustments and improvements that positively affect your score. Accuracy is the first step to credit restoration and good credit maintenance.

A consumer may make updates to their credit file by contacting the credit bureaus directly or registering online to manage file information. The resources for the three major credit bureaus are outlined on the following page.

Experian (800) 397-3742 www.experian.com
PO BOX 9701
Allen, TX 75013

Equifax (866) 349-5191 www.ai.equifax.com
475 Anton Blvd
Costa Mesa, CA 92626

Transunion (800) 916-8800
https://disputes.transunion.com
PO BOX 105281
Atlanta, GA 30348-5281

SAY NO TO FRAUD

Credit fraud has netted billions of dollars to thieves who take advantage of people by gaining sensitive credit information through various methods. When you take a proactive approach with protecting your credit file, you must be aware of the possibility that any type of personal data can be seamlessly stolen and used for the wrong purposes. One misstep could result in you becoming a victim of identity theft.

Credit thieves use many methods to obtain your vital information. These are a few that are most common.

Trash Picking: A credit thief will rifle through your trash to locate personal documents that you have carelessly thrown away. Bank statements, ATM receipts, tax returns, health documents, or anything that carries your social security number, dependents or date of birth should never be thrown away. These documents, if you have no use for them, should be shredded and then discarded. Invest in a small home shredder for added convenience or look up shredding centers in your city to destroy sensitive documents.

Mail Tampering: Anyone could conveniently reach inside of your mailbox to grab items that have been sent to your home, office, or other address. A credit card offer or convenience checks can be a jackpot for a thief looking for a quick opportunity to finance a few items in your name. Be sure to always keep your address updated with all creditors, employers, and banks you have. A bank statement could allow someone to see your whole account number and use it to pay bills by e-check. Additionally, if you live in an area where you feel your mail is not secure, invest in a post office box and have your mail forwarded there.

Leaving Your Purse or Wallet in Plain View: We keep a lot of things in our wallets and purses. Letting your personal items get out of your sight for even a small period of time can allow someone the opportunity to write down information or steal your items entirely. Many companies are not requiring a lot of information to be verified for online shopping nor is there a usual safety protocol set in place for many retail stores that accept payments through a credit card terminal. You should never leave your personal information in a place that is not secure. Also, you should not keep items such as your social security card, ATM Pin numbers, passports, or birth certificates within your wallet unless you are using them for an immediate purpose.

Email/Phone/Mailings: Fraudsters look for ways to convince you to provide them with your personal information through your email, phone, or through mail. A seemingly innocent email could have an attachment that will record your internet activity to obtain personal data. The person calling to tell you that you have won a contest you didn't enter doesn't have good intentions. Many recent claims have involved a person who claims to be calling from the IRS to collect on back taxes that are owed. Often, the caller will state that the tax payer may suffer severe consequences if a payment on their "tax liability" is not made before the end of the business day. It is not usual that the IRS will ever call you to collect a payment to any tax liabilities owed. In no instances should you pay anything or provide personal data without first researching the origin and validly of any calls that involve your financial well-being.

Skimming Machines: Skim machines are devices that are placed inside the card slot at places like the ATM, store, or any other place where you would use your credit card. These devices can retrieve your card number allowing anyone to obtain your credit/debit card information for them to use as they please. Fully check your ATM for tampering prior to using it.

"Phishing": Phishing describes a scam that is carried out regularly among the elderly or any other individual that cannot discern fraud attempts and may willingly exchange personal data over the phone or on the internet. A popular phishing scam involved many people receiving an email from PayPal. The email indicated that the user needed to "update" their PayPal accounts by providing personal details such as social security numbers and dates of birth. There were links that appeared to be valid along with a fully functioning website that had been set up to look like a valid PayPal account. Once the link was clicked and the victim has entered their information, a phisher gains access to the data and can use the data for their own purposes or sell it to the highest bidder.

Try to be aware of clues and when in doubt, do not give any personal financial details over the phone, email, or mail.

BRUISED CREDIT? HERE'S THE BAND-AID!

If you are seeking resources to view, clean and improve your credit, there are many free methods that allow you to take control of your personal information:

• **Letter Writing**: Sending letters through the mail seems to be something from ancient times. However, becoming a letter writer has advantages when it comes to your credit disputes. Be sure to write letters to creditors asking that they verify whether or not you owe an item in writing. Ask for proof of signatures, finance documents, etc. within your letters. Be sure to send this letter to an actual mailing address with either return receipt postage or certified mail. Retain a copy of these letters for yourself.

• **Follow Up**: Many of us have a great start when it comes to disputing our credit, however, when it comes to follow through, we fall short of the finish line. Set personal reminders for yourself to follow up weekly with creditors you've sent letters to. If you aren't receiving sufficient replies, escalate to management and notate names of the people you spoke to and their direct numbers if available. Many collection agencies require that notes be made if a consumer wishes to speak with a supervisor. The key is to be sure they document your calls on file.

• **Build Your Case**: Keep any relevant documentation you've received from a creditor and notate any piece of the conversation that you had concerning a document. When you've spent a few weeks and you haven't gotten anywhere with the creditor, you will need this documentation to prepare your dispute with the credit bureau. The goal is to let the credit bureau know that you have tried to resolve the error with the creditor and have been unsuccessful. By retaining your notes, names and contact numbers, the attempts you have made will be registered and the item may be removed entirely due to their lack of response or valid information.

• **Wash, Rinse, Repeat**: What your shampoo bottle says applies to credit. Make your credit repair activity a daily routine and if you receive a result that isn't what you expected, do not give up. The negative items that show up on your credit didn't happen overnight so clearing those items will not happen in a day. You must stay committed to your credit journey. Anything worth having is worth the work.

CREDIT READY? LET'S BUY A HOME!

Now that you have reversed your credit issues, it is time to focus on buying a home. Looking for a home requires you to ask the following questions to ensure you are preparing yourself for the home-buying process:

- Am I looking for a single family home, multi-unit property or condominium?
- Am I concerned with school districts, crime rates and or work commute?
- Am I going to stay in this town, state or country for the next 5 years?
- Do I want the responsibility of owning a home?

It is important to decide which sort of property you wish to buy since many loan products are restricted to a certain type of property.

A **single-family home** is the defined as any separately owned unit (not condo) that is sized for one family to live. This property type does not allow for illegal apartment improvements, etc.

Multi-Unit properties are comprised of real estate that may have two or more units. When purchasing this type of property, you must consider whether or not owning a building with multiple units is a responsibility you are willing to take on. As a landlord, you must be sure that you understand the regulation and laws protecting the rights of a tenant.

A **condominium** is a living space that is a part of several other units. The units are all governed by an association which is voted on by all owners in a complex. This condo association supervises the financial matter of the entire complex. This same association enforces rules that all occupants must comply with. Most condo associations require monthly payments be made for the upkeep and maintenance of common areas.

Aside from determining the type of home you wish to purchase, you must do research to ensure that you are seeking homes that fit your lifestyle. If you are a person who hates yard work, it may not make sense to buy a home that has a large lot. Also, if you prefer privacy, a dwelling like a condo may not suit your needs.

If you intend to relocate in a few years, then neither option may be good for you. It is important that you, as the consumer, investigate neighborhoods and reach out to local organizations to find out facts about the neighborhood.

WHICH LOAN IS RIGHT FOR ME?

Shopping for a home loan can be time-consuming and frustrating in some instances. However, educating yourself about the pros and cons of each product may save you a fortune in the long run. The main types of loans are either **Conventional** or **Government** loans.

Many years ago, a conventional loan meant that a home-buyer needed to put down at least 20 percent. Fortunately, times have changed and many loans provide flexibility that allows more people to buy a home. Now, with Private Mortgage Insurance (PMI), lenders can offer solutions that require less money down. This mortgage insurance is paid either monthly or is lumped into the loan. It covers the financial institution in the event a borrower forecloses on a property.

Depending on your financial situation, your lender may need to see several personal documents prior to determining which loan product may suit your needs. You should always have the following documents handy in order to begin the approval process:

- Last two years of W-2 forms, 1099, and/or unemployment statements.
- Last two years of filed Federal Income Tax Returns (all pages)
- Two recent pay stubs from your current employer.
- Two months of recent bank statements (all pages)
- Copy of ID or Driver's License
- Dates, names and addresses of all employers over the last two years.

It is important to provide truthful information during this process as failure to do so could result in your loan being denied. Your lender will most likely need to pull their own credit report.

If you provide all of the items needed, your lender should be able to get you a pre-approval for a home loan. This pre-approval is the document you need which will allow you to begin the process of looking at homes that are on the market to purchase. This pre-approval will also help determine which price range you must stay within for your new home.

You should always feel comfortable with asking your lender questions about the loan so that you fully understand the numbers. The most important questions to ask would be:

1. Does my loan have a pre-payment penalty?
2. Is the interest rate fixed?
3. How long will it take to process and close the loan?
4. How much money will I need for this process?
5. Are there any assistance programs that will help with down payment or closing costs?

Once you've determined that you are comfortable to move

forward, your lender will explore which options are available to you. Some loan types are discussed here:

Conventional Financing (Freddie or Fannie): This financing usually requires the borrower to put down 5% of the purchase price as a down payment. Some products allow for 3%. In some cases, your credit score must be over a certain range to qualify for this particular product. This loan may also require Private Mortgage Insurance (PMI) if you are unable to put 20 percent down. This loan requires an appraisal, or an evaluation of property, to determine if the home is worth what the seller is asking you to pay. This program can be used for the purchase of 1 to 4 units and/or condominiums.

FHA Financing: This particular loan is insured by the Department of Housing and Urban Development. An FHA loan allows a buyer to put 3.5% of the purchase price down. The credit score requirements may not always be as high as many conventional products. However, the loan does require that mortgage insurance be paid. Some of the fees are a bit higher with FHA as well but the interest rate is usually very competitive. This program does require an appraisal. You may purchase a property from 1 to 4 units using FHA financing. If you are interested in purchasing a condo using this program, your lender must determine if the condo association where the unit is located is FHA approved. If it is not, you may not move forward with financing that condo unit.

VA Financing: This product is reserved entirely for Veterans and/or their widows/widowers. This program doesn't require a minimum down payment and no monthly private mortgage insurance is required. A veteran may be exempt from certain fees if they have a service related disability. There are documents that a borrower must provide to determine VA eligibility (DD2-14, Certificate of Eligibility). This program does require an appraisal, and in many instances, a termite inspection is required. This program can also be used for 1 to 4 units and follows the same rule as FHA when it comes to condo units.

Once you have received your pre-approval letter, you may seek out a real estate professional to assist you in your home search. When selecting a Realtor, you need to know the following:

1. Are they familiar with the area in which you wish to buy?
2. Do they answer your questions in a way in which you can understand?
3. Do they listen to your concerns about price, repairs and location?
4. Are they available to set appointments within 24 hours?

MEET THE CONTRIBUTOR

Joy Sinegar-Munoz has over 17 years in the mortgage finance world. She obtained her Real Estate Agent License initially but then, after accompanying a friend to a Real Estate Mortgage Licensing class, Joy realized that her passion was funding the dream.

Joy's passion has earned her numerous awards and accolades from many in the industry. Her knowledge of rehabilitation concepts and credit repair have allowed her to help hundreds of people become homeowners and helped hundreds more save their homes through foreclosure counseling and refinance.

Raised in Joliet, Illinois, Joy decided to move to Chicago in order to reach borrowers who did not have the basic model of debt management, credit usage and real estate lending. After a decade, she has become well known as a leader in the Chicago market.

Joy still lives in Chicago, the community she serves, with her family. She enjoys music, motorcycling and travel.

CHAPTER 3:
DREAMING OF A PLACE OF YOUR OWN

By Wendy Lee

Have you been dreaming about wanting to own a place of your own? But you do not know where to start? Who to talk to? How to do it? Will I make the right decision? You might not have anyone to hold your hand through the process, spelling out the ABC's for first-time home buying.

Have no fear; we are here to help you sift through all of the big and little details. You have a team of professionals in the real estate industries here to walk you through the process. We have created a book for you that will walk you through the entire process. Instead of going to different resources, we have brought our all in one resource guide to you.

Together we help you accomplish your desire to become a homeowner.

Like everything else in the world, property rental prices are only going to continue to increase over time, so if you're tired of wasting your hard-earned paycheck month after month on rent: We got your back!

If you've consciously budgeted each month over the past however many years and have built up a significant savings, it might be time to consider buying. Yes. Become a homeowner. It might seem intimidating. But what do you really have to lose, but everything to gain by at least trying to explore that option. That way, we will know if buying property is still far off in the future for you, but it's imperative to get informed and start planning now so you'll know what to expect when the time comes.

The first and most essential step to undertake when you make the decision to buy a home is to wrap your head around the costs involved; this will likely mean developing and sticking to a budget.

Let's start with taking a look at your credit. Credit reports are kept by the three major credit agencies, Experian, Equifax, and

TransUnion. They show whether you are habitually late with payments and whether you have run into serious credit problems in the past. You have three different credit scores, one for each of your credit reports.

A low credit score may hurt your chances for getting the best interest rate, or getting financing at all. So at this point, I would suggest you contact a lender to pull your credit report to access your current financial status. The lender reports are the scores that you will need to base your action plan. The other resources, www.freeannualcreditreport.com and www.creditkarma.com
are only going to give a general idea of what your scores are.

Did you know that errors are common on your report? If you find any, contact the agencies directly to correct them, which can take two or three months to resolve. If the report is accurate but shows past problems, then be prepared to explain them to a loan officer. TELL THEM EVERYTHING!! PLEASE DO NOT TRY TO HIDE ANYTHING BECAUSE WHAT IS IN THE DARK DOES COME TO LIGHT!!!

Next topic. Have you set your budget? You will need to determine how much house you can afford. Contact your lender or ask your realtor for a referral, the loan officer will look at your income, debt, and credit to determine the kind of loan that fits your specific needs. There is no such thing as a one size fits all kind of loan out there. Some have great credit, some don't. Some are self-employed who file taxes with 1099 while there are those who have full/part-time employment, they file taxes with a W-2.

The rule of thumb is to aim for a home that costs about two-and-a-half times your gross annual salary. If you have significant credit card debt or other financial obligations like alimony, child support, student loans, then you may need to set your sights lower.

Another rule of thumb: All your monthly home payments should not exceed 36% of your gross monthly income. Depending on your credit, there are programs that can account for even up to 50% of gross monthly income, though we do not suggest you to consider buying until you have secured employment that will pay you more money, or another way to offset this higher debt to income ratio, by buying a multiple family dwelling. That way your tenants can help you supplement the mortgage.

Next step: You'll need to come up with cash for your down payment and closing costs. There are lender programs that need as little as 3% down. Gone are those days where you had to put 20% down. Of course, a lender would love to see that you can put 20% of purchase price down, but just know that there are many more options today than there was yesterday....

Various private and public agencies -- including Fannie Mae, Freddie Mac, the Federal Housing Administration, and the Department of Veterans Affairs -- provide low down payment mortgages through banks and mortgage companies. If you qualify, it's possible to pay as little as 3% up front.

Once you've considered the down payment, make sure you've got enough to cover fees and closing costs. These fees are involved appraisal fee, loan fees, attorney's fees, inspection, and the cost of a title search.

That is why it is so important that you have money in the bank, funds in your 401(k) that you withdraw from. The 401(k) administrator will allow you to pull funds from your retirement fund to purchase a home.

You can also obtain a gift from a family member, friend, or even from a settlement.

Next, let's find you a realtor. The best way to find one is to ask friends and family that have bought property before.

Some good questions to ask:

- How long have you been in business?
- How well do you know my neighborhoods of choice?

If their realtor did a great job for them, more than likely they will refer you to them. You need "exclusive buyer agent." All agents have access to the same MLS properties.

When connecting with your realtor, she/he will ask you a series of questions to access what you are looking for.

- Single family home
- Condominium/townhome (don't forget about those monthly assessments)
- Multiple family buildings.

Now the fun part begins…..looking for you a dream home.
Your first step here is to figure out what city or neighborhood you want to live in. Do your homework and research on your own about the neighborhoods/communities that are considered opportunity areas of growth and potential.

Make sure you set up- call or meeting with your realtor to set up a search of available properties in your targeted areas. The last thing you want to do is waste 30 minutes a day looking at properties which were never going to work for you–it gets frustrating very fast.

An agent will send you a list of properties in your targeted area via the MLS, Multiple Listing Service. You will then mark the properties you are interested in where you'll begin seeing places with your agent. Your agent's job is to schedule the appointments, make sure everything runs smoothly, and to answer questions you have. A good agent will know things like how much it would cost to add granite counters to your kitchen, replace kitchen or bath, or the approximate cost of utility services to properties such as yours. In general, they should be a great resource of knowledge that help you get educated and make the right decision. Depending on your schedule, the process of actually looking for a home can take from a few days to a month.

Things to keep on the top of mind when considering homes. Pay special attention to districts with good schools, even if you don't have school-age children. When it comes time to sell, you'll find that a strong school system is a major advantage in helping your home be more marketable. Make sure in making a final decision on your dream home, before you pull the trigger, we suggest you drive there and take a serious accounting of the other homes in the area.

Are they all well maintained? Are there transportation options readily available? Are there retail stores nearby? Make sure you drive in and around the neighborhood at different times of the day.

So are you ready to move to the next step? Once you find the house you want, move quickly to make your bid. Ask your realtor to pull comparative sales (as known as comps) in the area in the last 3-6 months. This will give you an idea if your home is worth the investment in comparison to the other sold homes. Your agent's job is to run numbers for you so you can both discuss what a reasonable purchase strategy is, basically in other words, how much to offer. This offer will then go into the seller's agent and negotiations will begin. Just as with the home search process, the time it takes to negotiate can vary wildly with some people taking hours and some days. Regardless of the timing, your agent and the other agent will go back and forth–with your permission- passing counters to one another until an agreement is reached. The updated contract is then sent to both parties for signatures and you are now officially under contract!

If you really want the house, don't lowball. A few extra thousand will not break the bank so do not lose your opportunity to secure the accepted contract!

In negotiating an offer, keep in mind of the current market conditions, hot seller's market or is it a hot buyer's market? Also this is a negotiation between buyer and seller, so do not lose sight that there is two parties to the transaction. The buyer wants the lowest price possible while the seller would like to get the most return from their investment.

Once you reach a mutually acceptable price, the seller's agent will draw up an offer to purchase that includes an estimated closing date. Buyer and seller will sign the offer, once both parties have signed, then we have an officially executed contract, a legal binding document between seller and buyer.

In writing an offer, make sure the deal is contingent upon your ability to secure a mortgage, doing an inspection with a licensed home inspector, not your friend or family that is a handyman, appraisal value covers the purchase print, and that your attorney review period is provided for.

Once you have a fully executed contract, it is time to contact the lender, attorney, and home inspector to do what they need to do.
Once under contract you have 4 major milestones to complete before you get the keys and officially become a homeowner: home inspection and attorney review, mortgage contingency, final walk through, and closing day.

In Illinois, buyers and sellers have the right to conduct an attorney review and inspection immediately following contract execution. During this period the buyer would pay for a licensed home inspector to come out to the home and give it a thorough inspection.

The home inspection can take anywhere from 2-3 hours depending on the size of the home.

It is suggested you be present during the inspection, because you will learn a lot about your house, including its overall condition, construction materials, wiring, any cosmetic defects, and most importantly info on all of the major structural items (roof, electrical, plumbing, windows). More than likely, the inspector will come up with a list of items that will need to be replaced or repaired, this applies to brand new homes as well……your realtor and/or attorney will prepare a list of repairs so that they can present to the seller side of transaction (listing agent and seller attorney). You will either want the seller to fix the problem before you move in, or deduct the cost of the repair from the final price. If the seller won't agree to either remedy, you may decide to walk away from the deal, which you can do without penalty if you have that contingency written into the contract. But keep in mind unless they are major structural issues, the seller may not have to make repairs on cosmetic items. Be selective with the list of repairs needed. Focus on making sure the major items will be addressed by seller.

The buyer and seller agree on what is being repaired/replaced.
Your attorney will have the right to approve, disapprove, or make

modifications to the contract. Just as with the inspection issues, the attorneys will go back and forth until an agreement is worked out. Once the attorney review and inspection period is signed off on, the next thing for you to focus on is the mortgage contingency. This part of the contract will call for you to have X amount of days to work with your lender to secure an unconditional mortgage commitment. This means that you have been approved for the loan subject to certain condition set forth by the lender. Your lender will typically need AT LEAST 30 days to get a mortgage and if you and your realtor try and make the closing happen quicker, you will likely run into problems. You will provide a lot of financial documents (W-2's, tax, and bank statements, debt documentation, tax returns) to your lender during this period and they will use those documents to work through the loan approval process for you.

At this time, lender will order an appraisal. This appraiser is sent out by the bank on your behalf to ensure that the money being loaned to you for the house is on par with the values. Over the next 2-3 weeks your loan application is in underwriting, working on securing your "clear to close." Once your loan is ready to close, you will waive your mortgage contingency and move on to the next step.

Okay so you've worked out all of the details of your deal and secured your financing–great–now it's time to conduct your final walk through in anticipation of closing. The final walk through exists so you and your realtor can lay eyes on the property as close as possible prior to closing to ensure no new issues have popped up and that any issues you and the seller agreed would be addressed have been. In most cases, everything will be fine, but occasionally something may not be done or a new issue has come up. If there are any outstanding issues –the attorneys and your realtor will still likely be able to work something out at the closing table to ensure you stay on track to close on time.

About two days before the actual closing, you will receive a final HUD Settlement Statement from your lender that lists all the charges you can expect to pay at closing.

Review it carefully. It will include all fees involved in the real estate transaction such as appraisal, application fee, credit report, attorney fees, commissions (paid by the seller), and title insurance. Title insurance protects you and the lender from any claims someone may make regarding ownership of your property.

Now the BIG DAY IS HERE!! CLOSING DAY!

Get a good night's rest. Because you will be moving the day off, or after the closing, make sure you connect with your realtor to do a final walk through, make sure that you account for everything you saw at the house is still there. The repairs that the seller agreed to address have been taken care. At the closing, you will be sitting with your attorney. They will go over and explain to you all of the forms you are signing.

Once everything is confirmed by your attorney, title representative (also called a closer), and lender, we wait for the wire transfer from your lender to hit the title company account. If all is agreed upon, and the funds have arrived, it is official, you are closed and a homeowner!!

Congratulations!! You are now a proud owner of a brand new home. Let's celebrate!

CHAPTER 4:
KEY QUESTIONS TO ASK YOUR HOME INSPECTOR

By Kevin Mathers

What to Ask Your Home Inspector. Don't be afraid to interview your potential inspector.

1) What does your inspection cover?
The inspector should ensure that their inspection and inspection report will meet all applicable requirements in your state if applicable and will comply with a well-recognized SOP, Standard of Practice and/or Code of Ethics.

2) How long have you been practicing in the home inspection profession and how many inspections have you completed?

The Inspector should be able to provide his or her history in the profession and even a few names as referrals. What type of homes have they inspected, newer, older, multi-unit?

3) How long will the inspection take?

The average inspection time will be between 2-3 hours for a typical single family home. Anything significantly less may not be enough time for a thorough inspection.

4) How much will it cost?
Cost can vary dramatically depending on size of property, age, services offered and even region. A typical range is from $300 to $500, but you should consider this value an investment being made. You can get what you pay for if you opt for a much lower inspection fee.

5) What type of inspection report do you provide and how long will it take to receive it?

Ask to see a sample report. Make sure you can understand the language and how detailed it is. Does it have pictures? Most inspectors can turn a report around in 24 hours.

6) Will I be able to attend the inspection?

It's highly recommended you attend. This is a valuable education opportunity, and ANY inspector that refuses your presents is a red flag.

7) Does the inspector maintain any membership with nationally recognized home inspection associations?

ASHI-American Society of Home Inspectors, InterNACHI-International Association of Certified Home Inspectors, AHIT-American Home Inspection Training. These are the top associations that have and require a SOP and Code of Ethics be followed.

8) Do you participate in continuing education programs to keep your expertise up to date?

One can never know it all, and the inspector's commitment to continuing education is critical in today's home market and the ever-changing requirements of a safe home.

These are some key questions you should ask along with any other that come to mind. If you have an inspector that cannot provide you with clear answers and is not willing to take the time to explain their protocol or willing to include you during the process, that would be a red flag.

Remember a home inspection is to provide the buyer with as much information as possible to make an informed decision. This is probably one of the largest investments a person will make in a lifetime and should not be taken lightly or looking for the best bottom line inspection fee.

KEY AREAS IN A HOME INSPECTION

Grounds Remarks

Service Walks/Driveways

Spalling concrete cannot be patched with concrete because the new will not bond with the old. Water will freeze between the two layers, or the concrete will break up from movement or wear. Replacement of the damaged section is recommended. Walks or driveways that are close to the property should be properly pitched away to direct water away from the foundation. Asphalt driveways should be kept sealed and larger cracks filled.

PATIOS

Patios that have settled towards the structure should be mud jacked or replaced to assure proper pitch. Improperly pitched patios are one source of wet basements/crawlspaces.

EXERIOR WOOD SURFACES

All surfaces of untreated wood need regular applications of paint or special chemicals to resist damage. Porch or deck columns and fence posts which are buried in the ground and made of untreated wood will become damaged within a year or two.

Decks that are not painted or stained should be treated with a water sealer as needed.

GRADING AND DRAINAGE

Any system of grading or landscaping that creates positive drainage (moving water away from the foundation walls) will help to keep a basement and crawlspace dry. Where negative grade exists and additional backfill is suggested, it may require digging out around the property to get a proper pitch. Dirt shall be approximately 6" below the bottom sill and should not touch wood surfaces.

Flower beds, loose mulched areas, railroad ties and other such landscaping items close to the foundation trap moisture and contribute to wet basements. To establish a positive grade, a proper slope away from the house is 1" per foot for approximately 5--6 feet. Recommend ground cover planting or grass up to foundation.

ROOF AND SURFACE WATER CONTROL

Roof and surface water must be controlled to maintain a dry basement and crawlspace. This means keeping gutters cleaned out, maintaining proper slope, extending downspouts, installing splash blocks, and building up the grade so that roof and surface water is diverted away from the building.

WINDOW WELLS

The amount of water which enters a window well from falling rain is generally slight, but water will accumulate in window wells if the yard is improperly graded. Plastic window well covers are useful in keeping out leaves and debris.

RETAINING WALLS

Retaining walls deteriorate because of excessive pressure buildup behind them, generally due to water accumulation. Conditions can often be improved by excavating a trench behind the retaining wall and filling it with coarse gravel. Drain holes through the wall will then be able to relieve the water pressure.

Retaining walls sometime suffer from tree root pressure or from general movement of topsoil down the slope. Normally, these conditions require rebuilding the retaining wall.

RAILINGS

It is recommended that railings be installed for any stairway over 3 steps and porches over 30" for safety reasons. Balusters for porches, balconies, and stairs should be close enough to assure children cannot squeeze through. Building standards are a maximum of 4" spacing between balusters.

Roof Remarks

Valleys and Flashings that are covered with shingles and/or tar or any other material are considered not visible.

Tar and Gravel Roofs - this type of covering on a pitched roof requires ongoing annual maintenance. We recommend that a roofing contractor evaluate this type of roof. Infra--red photography is best used to determine areas of potential leaks.

Flat roofs are very vulnerable to leaking. It is very important to maintain proper drainage to prevent the ponding of water. We recommend that a roofing contractor evaluate this type of roof.

ROOF TYPE	LIFE EXPECTANCY
Asphalt 3 tab Shingles	15--20 years
*Asphalt Multi--Thickness Shingles**	20--30 years
*Asphalt Interlocking. Shingles**	15--25 years
Asphalt Rolls	10 years
Built--up Roofing	10--20 years
*Wood Shingles**	10--40 years [1]
Clay *Tiles*,* *Cement*	2+ yea rs
*Slate Shingles**	30--100 years [2]
*Asbestos Cement Shingles**	30--75 years
Metal Roofing	15--40 + years
Single Ply Membrane	15--25 years
Polyurethane with Elastomeric Coating	10--40 years [1]

* Not recommended for use on low slope roof

1 Depending on local conditions and proper installation 2 Depending on quality of slate

Roof coverings should be visually checked in the spring and fall for any visible missing shingles, damaged coverings or other defects. Before re--roofing, the underside of the roof structure and roof sheathing should be inspected to determine that the roof structure can support the additional weight of the shingles.

Wood shakes and shingles will vary in aging, due to the quality of the material, installation, maintenance, and surrounding shade trees. Ventilation and drying of the wood material is critical in extending the life expectancy of the wood. Commercial preservatives are available on the market, which could be applied to wood to impede deterioration.

Exterior Remarks

CHIMNEYS

Chimneys built of masonry will eventually need tuck pointing. A cracked chimney top that allows water and carbonic acid to get behind the surface brick/stone will accelerate the deterioration. Moisture will also deteriorate the clay flue liner. Periodic chimney cleaning will keep you apprised of the chimney's condition. The flashing around the chimney may need resealing and should be inspected every year or two. Fireplace chimneys should be inspected and evaluated by a chimney professional before using. Chimneys must be adequate height for proper drafting. Spark arrestors are recommended for a wood burning chimney, and chimney caps for fossil fuels. Unlined Chimney -- should be re--evaluated by a chimney technician. Have flue cleaned and re--evaluated. The flue lining is covered with soot or creosote and no representation can be made as to the condition.

NOT EVALUATED

The flue was not evaluated due to inaccessibility such as roof pitch, cap, cleanout not accessible, etc.

CRICKET FLASHING

Small, sloped structure made of metal and designed to drain moisture away from a chimney. Usually placed at the back of a chimney. The latest building standards state a cricket flashing is required if the chimney chase is 30" or wider.

GUTTERS AND DOWNSPOUTS

This is an extremely important element in basement/crawlspace dampness control. Keep gutters clean and downspout extensions in place (6' or more). Paint the inside of galvanized gutters, which will extend the life. Shortly after a rain or thaw in winter, look for leaks at seams in the gutters. These can be recaulked before they cause damage to fascia or soffit boards. If no gutters exist, it is recommended that they be added.

SIDING

Wood siding should not come in contact with the ground. The moisture will cause rotting to take place and can attract carpenter ants. Brick and stone veneer must be monitored for loose or missing mortar. Some brick and stone are susceptible to spalling. This can be caused when moisture is trapped and a freeze/thaw situation occurs. There are products on the market that can be used to seal out the moisture. This holds true for brick and stone chimneys also. Metal siding will dent and scratch. Oxidation is a normal reaction in aluminum. There are good cleaners on the market and it is recommended that they be used occasionally. Metal siding can be painted.

EIFS

This type of siding is a synthetic stucco and has experienced serious problems. It requires a certified EIFS inspector to determine condition.

DOORS AND WINDOWS

These can waste an enormous amount of energy. Maintain the caulking around the frames on the exterior. Check for drafts in the winter and improve the worst offenders first. Windows that have leaky storm windows will usually have a lot of sweating. Likewise, well--sealed storms that sweat indicate a leaky window. It is the tighter unit that will sweat (unless the home has excess humidity to begin with).

Wood that exhibits blistering or peeling paint should be examined for possible moisture sources: roof leaks, bad gutters, interior moisture from baths or laundry or from a poorly vented crawl space. Some paint problems have no logical explanation, but many are a symptom of an underlying problem. A freshly painted house may mask these symptoms, but after you have lived in the home for a year or two, look for localized paint blistering (peeling).
New glazing will last longer if the raw wood is treated with boiled linseed oil prior to glazing. It prevents the wood from drawing the moisture out of the new glazing.

CAULKING

Many different types of caulk are available on the market today. Check with a paint or hardware store for the kind of application you need.

Electrical/A/C – Heat Pump Remarks

EXTERIOR DOORS

The exposed side of exterior wood doors needs to be painted or properly stained and varnished to prevent
discoloring and delamination. Weather--stripping is a must to prevent drafts.

ELECTRICAL

It is recommended that exterior receptacles be GFCI protected and that you test (and reset) them monthly. When you push the test button, the reset button should pop out, shutting off power to the receptacle. If it doesn't, the GFCI is not working properly. If you don't test them once a month, the GFCI receptacles have a tendency to stick and may not protect you when needed.

If you have overhead service conductors leading to the house they should be a minimum of 10' above walkways and the yard and 12' above driveways. Wires that are too low need to be repaired either by the power company or a qualified licensed electrical contractor.

A/C –HEAT PUMP

The circuit breakers to A/C should be on for a minimum of 24 hours and the outside temperature at least 60 degrees for the past 24 hours or an A/C system otherwise potential damage to the system may occur. We recommend checking the instructions in your A/C manual before starting the unit up in summer. A heat pump should only be tested in the mode it's running in. Outside temperature should be at least 65 degrees for the past 24 hours to run in cooling mode.

Temperature differential in the cooling mode that is between 14--22 degrees, is usually acceptable. If this is out of range, have an HVAC contractor examine it. It isn't always feasible to do a temperature differential due to high humidity, low outside temperature, etc.

A/C CONDENSOR COIL

They should be kept clear from overgrown foliage. Clearance requirements vary, but 2' on all sides should be considered minimal with up to 6' of air discharge desirable. If clothes dryers vent within 5--10', either relocate the vent or do not run the dryer when the A/C is running. The lint can quickly reduce the efficiency of the A/C unit.

Garage/Carport Remarks

OVERHEAD DOOR OPENERS

We recommend that a separate electrical outlet be provided. Openers that do not have a safety reverse are considered a safety hazard. Small children and pets are especially vulnerable. We recommend the operating switches be set high enough so children cannot reach them. If an electric sensor is present, it should be tested occasionally to ensure it is working.

GARAGE SILL PLATES

Garage sill plates should be elevated or treated lumber should be used. If this is not the case, periodically monitor the sill plates for damage.

BURNERS

Any appliance such as a water heater, furnace, etc. should have the flame a minimum of 18" above the floor. Any open flame less than 18" from the floor is a potential safety hazard. The appliance should also be protected from vehicle damage. Elevation of the ignition source is not required for appliances that are listed as flammable vapor ignition resistant.

Water Heaters

Many electric water heaters thermostats have enclosed contacts, but they are not sealed gas tight. Therefore if an electric water heater unit with an ignition source located less than 18" from the bottom of the unit, it is required that the unit be elevated so the ignition source is at least 18" above the garage floor. Electric water heaters having all switching controls above 18" from the bottom of the water heater are not required to be elevated.

Interior Kitchen Remarks

PLASTER ON WOOD LATH

Plaster on wood lath is an old technique and is no longer in general use. Wood lath shrinks with time and the nails rust and loosen. As a result, the plaster may become fragile and caution is needed in working with this type of plastering system. Sagging ceilings are best repaired by laminating drywall over the existing plaster and screwing it to the ceiling joists.

PLASTER ON GYPSUM LATH (ROCK LATH)

Plaster on gypsum lath will sometimes show the seams of the 16" wide gypsum lath, but this does not indicate a structural fault.

WOOD FLOORING

Always attempt to clean wood floors first before making the decision to refinish the floor. Wax removers and other mild stripping agents plus a good waxing and buffing will usually produce satisfactory results. Mild bleaching agents help remove deep stains. Sanding removes some of the wood in the floor and can usually be done safely only once or twice in the life of the floor, depending on the wood thickness. Wood laminate floors cannot be sanded.

NAIL POPS

Drywall nail pops are due to normal expansion and contraction of the wood members to which the drywall is nailed and are usually of no structural significance. In newer homes and remodels they use screws instead of nails so nail popping is becoming less common in homes.

CARPETING

Where carpeting has been installed, the materials and condition of the floor underneath cannot be determined.

APPLIANCES

(If report indicated appliances were operated, the following applies) Dishwashers are tested to see if the motor operates and water sprays properly. Stoves are tested to see that burners are working and that the oven and broiler get hot. Timer and controls are not tested. Refrigerators are not tested. Most new Dishwashers have the drain line looped automatically and may not be visible on the day of inspection. It is essential for the dishwasher drain line to have an anti--siphon break to prevent backflow. A drain line loop or Dishwasher air gap should be installed if found to be missing. No representation is made to continued life expectancy of any appliance.

ASBESTOS AND OTHER HAZARDS

Asbestos fibers in some form are present in many older homes, but are often not visible and cannot be identified without testing.
If there is reason to suspect that asbestos may be present and if it is of particular concern, a sample of the material in question may be removed and analyzed in a laboratory. However, detecting or inspecting for the presence or absence of asbestos is not a part of our inspection.
Also excluded from this inspection and report are the possible presence of, or danger from, radon gas, lead--based paint, urea formaldehyde, toxic or flammable chemicals and all other similar or potentially harmful substances and environmental hazards.

WINDOWS

A representative number of windows are inspected.

Bathroom(s) Remarks

STALL SHOWER

A metal shower pan in a stall shower has a potential or probable life of 10--20 years depending on quality of the pan installed. Although a visible inspection is made to determine whether a shower pan is currently leaking, it cannot be stated with certainty that no defect is present or that one may not soon develop. Shower pan leaks often do not show except when the shower is in actual use. New shower pans use a waterproof material underneath that doesn't have the same problems as the older metal shower pans.

CERAMIC TILE

Bathroom tile installed in a mortar bed is excellent. It is still necessary to keep the joint between the tile and the tub/shower caulked or sealed to prevent water spillage from leaking through and damaging the ceilings below.

Ceramic tile is often installed in mastic. It is important to keep the tile caulked or water will seep behind the tile and cause deterioration in the wallboard. Special attention should be paid to the area around faucets and other tile penetrations.

EXHAUST FANS

Bathrooms with a shower should have exhaust fans when possible. This helps to remove excess moisture from the room, preventing damage to the ceiling and walls and wood finishes. The exhaust fan should not be vented into the attic. The proper way to vent the fan(s) is to the outside. Running the vent pipe horizontally and venting into a gable end or soffit with a proper end fitting is preferred. Running the vent pipe vertically through the roof may cause condensation to run down the vent pipe, rusting the fan and damaging the wallboard. Insulating the vent pipe in the attic will help to reduce this problem. If there isn't a fan an operable window is also acceptable by the current building standards.

SLOW DRAINS

Slow drains on sinks, tubs, and showers are usually due to buildup of hair and soap scum. Most sink
popups can be easily removed for cleaning. Some tubs have a spring attached to the closing lever that acts as a catch for hair. It may require removing a couple of screws to disassemble. If you cannot mechanically remove the obstruction, be kind to your pipes. Don't use a caustic cleaner. There are several bacteria drain cleaners available. They are available at hardware stores in areas where septic tanks are used. These drain cleaners take a little longer to work, but are safe for you and your pipes.

SAFETY HAZARDS

Typical safety hazards found in bathrooms are open grounds or reverse polarity by water. Installing outlets with G.F.C.I.'s are recommended.

WHIRLPOOL TUBS

This relates to interior tubs hooked up to interior plumbing. Where possible, the motor will be operated to see that the jets are working. Hot tubs and spas are not inspected. There should also be an easy to access panel that can be removed to gain access to the motor and the motor cord plugged into a GFCI protected outlet.

Interior Room(s) Remarks

DOOR STOPS

All swinging doors should be checked for door stops. Broken or missing door stops can result in door knobs breaking through drywall or plaster.

CLOSET GUIDES

Sliding closet doors should be checked to see that closet guides are in place. Missing or broken closet guides can cause scratches and damage to doors.

COLD AIR RETURNS

Bedrooms that do not have cold air returns in them should have a 3/4" gap under the doors to allow cold air to be drawn into the hall return.

AN INSPECTION VERSUS A WARRANTY

A home inspection is just what the name indicates, an inspection of a home...usually a home that is being purchased. The purpose of the inspection is to determine the condition of the various systems and structures of the home. While an inspection performed by a competent inspection company will determine the condition of the major components of the home, no inspection will pick up every minute latent defect. The inspector's ability to find all defects is limited by access to various parts of the property, lack of information about the property and many other factors. A good inspector will do his or her level best to determine the condition of the home and to report it accurately. The report that is issued is an opinion as to the condition of the home. This opinion is arrived at by the best technical methods available to the home inspection industry. It is still only an opinion.

A warranty is a policy sold to the buyer that warrants that specific items in the home are in sound condition and will remain in sound condition for a specified period of time. Typically, the warranty company never inspects the home. The warranty company uses actuarial tables to determine the expected life of the warranted items and charges the customer a fee for the warranty that will hopefully cover any projected loss and make a profit for the warranty seller. It is essentially an insurance policy.
The service that we have provided you is an inspection. We make no warranty of this property. If you desire warranty coverage, please see your real estate agent for details about any warranty plan to which their firm may have access.

WINDOW FRAMES AND SILLS

Window frames and sills are often found to have surface deterioration due to condensation that has run off the window and damaged the varnish. Usually this can be repaired with a solvent style refinisher and fine steel wool. This is sometimes a sign of excess humidity in the house. See comments regarding caulking doors and windows.

FIREPLACES

It is important that a fireplace be cleaned on a routine basis to prevent the buildup of creosote in the flue, which can cause a chimney fire. Masonry fireplace chimneys are normally required to have a terra cotta flue liner or 8 inches of masonry surrounding each flue in order to be considered safe and to conform with most building codes. During visual inspections, it is not uncommon to be unable to detect the absence of a flue liner either because of stoppage at the firebox, a defective damper or lack of access from the roof. Creosote buildup is common with wood burning fireplaces if not cleaned annually and the fireplace is used often. Metal Flues are also acceptable that service a fireplace.

WOODBURNERS

Once installed, it can be difficult to determine proper clearances for wood burning stoves. Manufacturer specifications, which are not usually available to the inspector, determine the proper installation. We recommend you ask the owner for paperwork, verifying that it was installed by a professional contractor.

VENTILATION

Ventilation is recommended at the rate of one square foot of vent area to 300 square feet of attic floor space, this being divided between soffit and rooftop. Power vents should ideally have both a humidistatand a thermostat, since ventilation is needed to remove winter moisture as well as summer heat. Evidence of condensation such as blackened roof sheathing, frost on nail heads, etc. is an indication that ventilation may have been or is blocked or inadequate.

INSULATION

The recommended insulation in the attic area is R--38 but varies depending on where you live, if the insulation is fiberglass approximately 12--17". If insulation is added, it is important that the ventilation is proper.

SMOKE DETECTORS

Smoke detectors should be tested monthly. At least one detector should be on each level, ideally in each bedroom as well. CO detectors are highly recommended.

VAPOR BARRIERS

The vapor barrier should be on the warm side of the surface(depending where you live.) Most older homes were built without vapor barriers. If the vapor barrier is towards the cold side of the surface, it should be sliced or removed. Most vapor barriers in the attic are covered by insulation and therefore, not visible.

SAFETY GLAZING

Safety glazing requirements vary depending on the age of the home. Every attempt is made to identify areas where the lack of safety glazing presents an immediate safety hazard, such as a shower door. In some older homes it is difficult to determine if safety glazing is present, since the glass is not marked. Therefore, no representation is made that safety glazing exists in all appropriate areas.

INSULATED GLASS

Broken seal in thermo pane/insulated windows are not always visible nor detectible due to humidity and temperature changes during the day. Other factors such as window covering, dirty windows, and lack of accessibility, personal property placed in front of the windows all affect the view of the windows at the time of the inspection.

Basement Remarks

BASEMENT/CRAWLSPACE

Most block basements/crawlspace has step cracks in various areas. If little or no movement has occurred and the step cracks, are uniform, this is considered acceptable. Horizontal cracks in the third or fourth block down indicate the block has moved due to outside pressure. They can be attributed to many factors such as improper grading, improperly functioning gutter and downspout system, etc. Normally if little or no movement has taken place and proper grading and downspouts exist, this is considered acceptable. If the wall containing the stress crack(s) has moved considerably, this will require some method of reinforcement. Basements/crawlspace that have been freshly painted or tuck pointed should be monitored for movement. This will be indicated by cracks reopening. If cracks reappear, reinforcement may be necessary. Reinforcing a basement/crawlspace wall can become expensive.

FOUNDATION (COVERED WALLS)

Although an effort has been made to note any major inflections or weaknesses, it is difficult at best to detect these areas when walls are finished off, or basement/crawlspace storage makes areas inaccessible. No representation is made as to the condition of these walls.

INSULATED CONCRETE FORMS (ICF'S)

ICF's are formwork for concrete that stays in place as permanent building insulation for energy--efficient, cast--in-- place, reinforced concrete walls, floors and roofs.

MONITOR

Indicates that the walls have stress cracks, but little movement has occurred. In our opinion, the cracks should be filled with mortar and the walls monitored for further movement and cracking. If additional movement or cracking occurs, reinforcement may be necessary.

HAVE EVALUATED

We recommend that the walls be re--evaluated by a structural engineer or basement/crawlspace repair company and estimates be obtained if work is required.

VAPOR BARRIER

Floors that are dirt or gravel should be covered with a vapor barrier and properly sealed.

MOISTURE PRESENT

Basement/crawlspace dampness is frequently noted in houses and in most cases the stains, moisture or efflorescence present is a symptom denoting that a problem exists outside the home. Usual causes are improper downspout extensions or leaking gutters and/or low or improper grade (including concrete surfaces) at the perimeter of the house. A proper slope away from the house is one inch per foot for five to six feet. No representation is made to future moisture that may appear.

PALMER VALVE

Many older homes have a valve in the floor drain. This drain needs to remain operational.

DRAIN TILE

We offer no opinion about the existence or condition of the drain tile, as it cannot be visibly inspected.

BASEMENT ELECTRICAL OUTLETS

We recommend that you have an outlet within 6' of each appliance. The appliance you plan to install may be different than what exists; therefore the inspection includes testing a representative number of receptacles that exist. It is also recommended to have ground fault circuit interrupters for any outlet in the unfinished part of the basement and crawl spaces. Except for outlets where the sump pump is plugged into.

Crawlspace Remarks

CRAWL SPACES

Crawl spaces are shallow spaces between the first level floor joist and the ground. Access to this area may be from the inside, outside or not accessible at all. Ductwork, plumbing, and electrical may be installed in the space in which access may be necessary. The floor of the crawl space may be covered with concrete, gravel, or may be the original soil. A vapor barrier may be a sheet of plastic or tar paper and installed over or under this material. The vapor barrier will deter the moisture from the earth from escaping into the crawl space and causing a musty smell. Every attempt is made to determine if paneling is warped, moisture stains are bleeding through, etc. Storage that blocks the visibility of a wall is not removed to examine that area. Therefore, it is important that on your walk-- through before closing, you closely examine these areas. There is debate about crawlspace ventilation; we recommend you contact a basement contractor for advice.

HAVE EVALUATED

We recommend that the walls be re--evaluated by a structural engineer or basement repair company and estimates be obtained if work is required.

MONITOR

Indicates that the walls have stress cracks, but little movement has occurred. In our opinion, the cracks should be filled with mortar and the walls monitored for further movement and cracking. If additional movement or cracking occurs, reinforcement may be necessary.

FOUNDATION (COVERED WALLS)

Although an effort has been made to note any major inflections or weaknesses, it is difficult at best to detect these areas when walls are finished off, or basement/crawlspace storage makes areas inaccessible. No representation is made as to the condition of these walls.

MOISTURE PRESENT

Basement/crawlspace dampness is frequently noted in houses and in most cases the stains, moisture or efflorescence present is a symptom denoting that a problem exists outside the home. Usual causes are improper downspout extensions or leaking gutters and/or low or improper grade (including concrete surfaces) at the perimeter of the house. A proper slope away from the house is one inch per foot for four to six feet. No representation is made to future moisture that may appear.

Plumbing Remarks

WELLS

Examination of wells is not included in this visual inspection. It is recommended that you have well water checked for purity by the local health authorities and, if possible, a check on the flow of the well in periods of drought. A well pit should have a locked cover on it to prevent anyone from falling into the pit.

SEPTIC SYSTEMS

The check of septic systems is not included in our visual inspection. You should have the local health authorities or other qualified experts check the condition of the septic system. In order for the septic system to be checked, the house must have been occupied within the last 30 days.

WATER PIPES

Galvanized water pipes rust from the inside out and may have to be replaced within 20 to30 years. This is usually done in two stages: horizontal piping in the basement first, and vertical pipes throughout the house later as needed. Copper pipes usually have more life expectancy and may last as long as 60 years or more before needing to be replaced.

HOSE BIBS

During the winter months it is necessary to make sure the outside faucets are winterized. This can be done by means of a shut--off valve located in the basement or crawlspace. Leave the outside faucets open to allow any water standing in the pipes to drain, preventing them from freezing. Hose bibs cannot be tested when winterized. Hoses should always be disconnected in winter, in cold climates.

WATER HEATER

The average life expectancy of a water heater is 5--10 years. Water heaters generally need not be replaced unless they leak. It is a good maintenance practice to drain 5--10 gallons from the heater several times a year. Missing relief valves or improper extension present a safety hazard. The temperature/pressure valve should be tested several times a year by lifting the valve's handle. Caution: very hot water will be discharged. If no water comes out, the valve is defective and must be replaced.

WATER SOFTENERS

During a visual inspection it is not possible to determine if water is being properly softened.

SHUT--OFF VALVES

Most shut--off valves have not been operated for long periods of time. We recommend operating each shut--off valve to: toilet bowl, water heater, under sinks, main shut--off, hose faucets, and all others. We recommend you have a plumber do this, as some of the valves may need to be repacked or replaced. Once the valves are in proper operating order, we recommend opening and closing these valves several times a year.

POLYBUTYLENE PIPING

This type of piping has a history of problems and should be examined by a licensed plumber and repaired or replaced as necessary.

MECHANICAL DEVICES MAY OPERATE AT ONE MOMENT AND LATER MALFUNCTION; THEREFORE, LIABILITY IS SPECIFICALLY LIMITED TO THOSE SITUATIONS WHERE IT CAN BE CONCLUSIVELY SHOWN THAT THE MECHANICAL DEVICE INSPECTED WAS INOPERABLE OR IN THE IMMEDIATE NEED OF

REPAIR OR NOT PERFORMING THE FUNCTION FOR WHICH IS IT WAS INTENDED AT THE TIME OF INSPECTION.

CSST

Corrugated Stainless Steel Tubing is an alternative to traditional black iron gas piping. It is a continuous, flexible, stainless steel pipe with an exterior PVC covering. Many areas of the country require that CSST be continuous and directly bonded to the electrical ground system of the premises in which it was installed.

Heating System Remarks

HEATING AND AIR CONDITIONING units have limited lives. Normal lives are:

Approximate Age GAS--FIRED HOT AIR
OIL--FIRED HOT AIR
CAST IRON BOILER (Hot water or steam) or more

STEEL BOILER (Hot water or steam)

COPPER BOILER (Hot water or steam)

CIRCULATING PUMP (Hot water)
AIR CONDITIONING COMPRESSOR HEAT PUMP

15--25 years 20--30 years 30--50 years

30--40 years

10--20 years

10--15 years 8--12 years 8--12 years

Gas--fired hot air units that are close to or beyond their normal lives have the potential of becoming a source of carbon monoxide in the home. You may want to have such a unit checked every year or so to assure yourself that it is still intact. Of course a unit of such an age is a good candidate for replacement with one of the new, high efficiency furnaces. The fuel savings alone can be very attractive.

Boilers and their systems may require annual attention. If you are not familiar with your system, have a heating contractor come out in the fall to do routine maintenance. Caution: do not add water to a hot boiler!

Forced air systems should have filters changed every 30 to 60 days of the heating and cooling season. This is especially true if you have central air conditioning. A dirty air system can lead to premature failure of your compressor -- a $1,500 component.

Oil--fired furnaces and boilers should be serviced by a professional each year. Most experts agree you will pay for the service cost in fuel saved by having a properly tuned burner.

Read the instructions for maintaining the humidifier on your furnace. A malfunctioning humidifier can rust out a furnace rather quickly. It is recommended that the humidifier be serviced at the same time as the furnace, and be cleaned regularly. During a visual inspection it is not possible to determine if the humidifier is working.

Have HVAC technician examine -- a condition was found that suggests a heating contractor should do a further analysis. We suggest doing this before closing.

Heat exchangers cannot be examined nor their condition determined without being disassembled. Since this is not possible during a visual, non--technically exhaustive inspection, you may want to obtain a service contract on the unit or contact a furnace technician regarding a more thorough examination.

Testing pilot safety switch requires blowing out the pilot light. Checking safety limit controls requires disconnecting blower motor or using other means beyond the scope of this inspection. If the furnace has not been serviced in last 12 months you may want to have a furnace technician examine.

CO Test -- this is not part of a non--technical inspection. If a test was performed, the type of tester is indicated.

Combustible Gas Detector -- if a gas detector was used during the inspection of the furnace and evidence of possible combustible gases was noted, we caution you that our test instrument is sensitive to many gases and not a foolproof test. None--the--less, this presents the possibility that a hazard exists.

A/C CONDENSER COIL

They should not become overgrown with foliage. Clearance requirements vary, but 2' on all sides should be considered minimal with up to 6' of air discharge desirable. If a clothes dryer vent is within five to ten feet, either relocate the vent or do not run when the A/C is running. The lint will quickly reduce the efficiency of the A/C unit.

Electrical/Cooling Remarks

Every effort has been made to evaluate the size of the service. Three wires going into the home indicates 240 volts. The total amperage can be difficult to determine. We highly recommend that ground fault circuit interrupters (G.F.C.I.) be connected to all outlets around water. This device automatically shuts the circuit off when it senses a current leak to ground. This device can be purchased in most hardware stores. G.F.C.I.'s are recommended by all outlets located near water, outside outlets, or garage outlets. Pool outlets should also be protected with a G.F.C.I. See diagram below:

If you do have G.F.C.I.'s, it is recommended that you test (and reset) them monthly. When you push the test button, the reset button should pop out, shutting off the circuit. If it doesn't, the breaker is not working properly. If you don't test them once a month, the breakers have a tendency to stick and may not protect you when needed.

Knob and tube wiring found in older homes should be checked by an electrician to insure that the wire cover is in good condition. Under no circumstances should this wire be covered with insulation. Recess light fixtures that are not IC-- Rated should have a baffle around them so that they are not covered with insulation. The newer recessed fixtures will shut off if they overheat. (no representation is made as to proper recess lighting fixtures).

Federal Pacific Stab--Lok® Electrical panels may be unsafe. See www.google.com (Federal Pacific) Aluminum wiring in general lighting circuits has a history of problems, with the potential of a fire. If this type of wiring exists, a licensed electrical contractor should examine the whole system.

Arc Faults
In some areas arc faults are required in new homes, starting in 2002 and these control outlets in the bedrooms. In some areas arc faults are required for all 120 Volt circuits that are not GFCI protected in new homes starting in 2009.
Upgraded as desired for enhanced safety. Requirements will vary, across the US.

Cooling
Testing A/C System and Heat Pump-- The circuit breakers to A/C should be on for a minimum of 24 hours and the outside temperature at least 60 degrees for the past 24 hours or an A/C system cannot be operated without possible damage to the compressor. Check the instructions in your A/C manual or on the outside compressor before starting up in the summer. Heat pump can only be tested in the mode it's running in. Outside temperature should be at least 65° for the past 24 hours to run in cooling mode. Temperature differential, between 14°--22°, is usually acceptable. If out of this range, have an HVAC contractor examine it. It is not always feasible to do a differential test due to high humidity, low outside temperature, etc.

PREVENTIVE MAINTENANCE TIPS

I. FOUNDATION&MASONRY:

Basements, Exterior Walls: To prevent seepage and condensation

problems. a. Check basement for dampness & leakage after wet weather.
b. Check chimneys, deteriorated chimney caps, loose and missing mortar. c. Maintain grading sloped away from foundation walls.

II. ROOFS&GUTTERS:

To prevent roof leaks, condensation, seepage and decay problems.
a. Check for damaged, loose or missing shingles, blisters.
b. Clean gutters, leaders, strainers, window wells, drains. Be sure downspouts direct water away from foundation. Cut back tree limbs.
c. Check flashings around roof stacks, vents, skylights, chimneys, as sources of leakage. Check vents, louvers and chimneys for birds' nests, squirrels, insects.
d. Check fascias and soffits for paint flaking, leakage & decay.

III. EXTERIORWALLS:

To prevent paint failure, decay and moisture penetration problems.
a. Check painted surface for paint flaking or paint failure. Cut back shrubs.
b. Check exterior masonry walls for cracks, looseness, missing or broken mortar.

IV. DOORSAND WINDOWS:

To prevent air and weather penetration problems.
a. Check caulking for decay around doors, windows, corner boards, joints. Recaulk and weather-stripping as needed. Check glazing, putty around windows.

V. ELECTRICAL:

For safe electrical performance, mark & label each circuit.
a. Trip circuit breakers every six months and ground fault circuit interrupters (G.F.C.I.) monthly.
b. Check condition of lamp cords, extension cords & plugs. Replace at first sign of wear & damage. c. Check exposed wiring & cable for wear or damage.
d. If you experience slight tingling shock from handling or touching any appliance, disconnect the appliance & have it repaired. If lights flicker or dim, or if appliances go on and off unnecessarily, call a licensed electrician.

VI. PLUMBING:

For preventive maintenance.

a. Drain exterior water lines, hose bibs, sprinklers, pool equipment in the fall.

b. Draw off sediment in water heaters monthly or per manufacturer's instructions. c. Have septic tank serviced every 2 years.

VII. HEATING&COOLING:

For comfort, efficiency, energy conservation and safety.

a. Change or clean furnace filters, air handler filters, electronic filters as needed. b. Clean and service humidifier. Check periodically and annually.

c. Have oil burning equipment serviced annually.

VIII. INTERIOR:

General house maintenance.

a. Check bathroom tile joints, tub grouting & caulking. Be sure all tile joints in bathrooms are kept well sealed with tile grout to prevent damage to walls, floors & ceilings below.

b. Check underside of roof for water stains, leaks, dampness & condensation, particularly in attics and around chimneys.

IX. Know the location of:

- Main water shutoff valve.
- Main electrical disconnect or breaker.
- Main emergency shutoff switch for the heating system.

MEET THE CONTRIBUTOR

Kevin Mathers provides home inspection reporting for homeowners buying, selling or remaining to determine areas of repair and safety concerns. Detailed visual and testing of all components of the home. kgmhomeinspection.com

CHAPTER 5: NEGOTIATING YOUR CONTRACT

By Yondi K. Morris-Andrews

Purchasing a home can be a very daunting experience. But, have no fear! As long as you have a great team on your side, you will be guided through the entire experience and for the most part, enjoy your journey to homeownership! So, why do you need an attorney you ask? Great question! Purchasing a home is one of the biggest investments you will make in your lifetime, so having a real estate attorney review your contract, negotiate the items from your inspection report that the seller will repair, reviewing your title, and assisting you on the day of closing is pertinent. Here is your step by step guide for the role your attorney will have throughout your home buying experience.

Once your real estate agent presents an offer on your behalf and the offer is accepted by the seller, you have what's called an "Executed Contract." Your contract is pretty standard, but there are some things that an attorney will likely want to change or add to the contract on your behalf. You have exactly five business days to have your attorney review your contract and have changes made. It's very important to secure your attorney right at the onset of your contract being executed so that you don't miss your deadline to request changes!

During this five day period, it's also very important that you have an inspection conducted on the property. Even if the property looks like pure gold, there can be defects that are hidden that you can't see. An experienced inspector will take a few hours to go through the property and locate any and everything that could need to be replaced or repaired. This step is so crucial as you want to know if this new investment is a good one or a money pit! Once your inspector has completed the inspection, you will be given an inspection report. This report will provide you with a host of information about the property and most important, will give you an idea of what needs to be repaired. This is where your attorney steps in again. Your attorney and your agent will go over this inspection report with you so that together, you can determine what items you wish to present to the seller for them to repair on your behalf.

Here is where true negotiating can come into play. The seller often does not want to replace or repair everything. From the seller's perspective, they feel like they are selling their home and the last thing they want to do is have to make repairs. But, usually they are willing to make some repairs unless the purchase was executed "as is." Your attorney will ask you which items on the inspection report are most important to you. At that point, your attorney will ask the seller to repair the items that you care about the most and often throw in a couple more things for good measure! Usually it takes a few days for the seller's attorney to respond as they are determining what the cost might be for them to make these repairs. Most often, they respond with a yes to some items and a no to other items. At that point, it's time for your agent and you to have a chat and determine what you think is fair.

There are some instances in which the seller doesn't want to make repairs; rather they are willing to give you a credit to make those repairs on your own. This works well for some buyers as they want to hire their own contractors to make repairs. In this situation, your attorney and the seller's attorney will determine a dollar amount that the seller will provide you at closing so that you can have your repairs done, post-closing, on your own.

Once your attorney is finished negotiating your contract and the inspection items, you will be working with your lender (bank) to get all items submitted for your loan approval. This is the longest part of the process. There are lots of various documents that your lender is going to request from you, and the sooner you get those items submitted, the better! The attorney's job during this time is to check in with your lender weekly to see how your loan application is coming along. There are instances in which a buyer might need additional time to get the loan approved, so your attorney will have to communicate that to the seller's attorney so that everyone is always on the same page. One of the most important aspects of this process is communication! All parties need to be communicating often and your attorney should be there to answer any and every question that you might have.

Once you have submitted everything to your lender and your

loan officer approves your loan, you will hear this magic phrase "Clear to Close." That is when you can begin to celebrate as you are now almost ready to close on your home! At that point, your lender will issue you a closing disclosure (referred to as a CD), which will list all of the fees that you can expect to pay at closing. Commonly, people will say this is the "bottom line figure that you have to bring to the closing table." The day before closing, your lender and your attorney will confirm that total amount that you are to bring with you, either via a cashier's check or wire, to the title company. The title company is the office that you will be in on closing day!

So, now you've made it through everything! You've negotiated your contract and inspection issues, you've gone through the entire loan approval process and passed with flying colors and now you are at the closing table! On your closing day, you will be signing a lot of documents, or as some people like to say, signing your life away! No fear! All of the documents that you will sign will be standard. The most important ones you will see are the mortgage, the note, your closing disclosure, and your deed. It takes about an hour for your attorney to explain all of the documents to you that you will sign, but that's the great thing about having an attorney; they are there to read everything for you and can paraphrase what is inside of the documents so that you feel knowledgeable about what you are signing! The attorney will also review title to your property to make sure there are no liens or violations on the property. After you finish signing the documents, the person at the title company who has been assisting you will scan all of your documents and send them to your bank. The bank wants to make sure that no signatures have been missed and that you are good to go. You can expect to be at the closing from about 2-3 hours. Once the title company says okay, we are good to go; it's time to pop your bottle of champagne as you are now a homeowner! Your agent will likely be there to greet you with a hug and you will get the keys to your new home! And, you will have learned so much about the home buying process that you can help all of your friends and family when it's their turn! Congratulations!!!

MEET THE CONTRIBUTOR

Yondi K. Morris-Andrews
Founding Partner of Knight, Morris & Reddick Law Group

Yondi K. Morris-Andrews is a founding partner of Knight, Morris & Reddick Law Group. She specializes in various practice areas including real estate transactions, corporate and entertainment. With her real estate clients, Morris-Andrews represents clients in the buying and selling of both residential and commercial properties. Morris-Andrews works closely with clients and agents on her deals, and as a Chicago native, has insight regarding various neighborhoods and what her clients should consider when buying or selling their home. Morris-Andrews holds her client's hands every step of the way, making sure they understand the entire process and feel comfortable as they embark on likely one of the largest investments of their lives. Her real estate clients include first time homebuyers, sellers, investors and developers.

With her corporate clients, Morris-Andrews works mostly with start-up companies, offering them advice on how to form as an entity, while drafting and negotiating contracts on the company's behalf. Morris-Andrews offers creative solutions for her entrepreneur clients, and is able to guide them as they grow from the start-up phase to experienced businesses. She has been hired by her clients to act as general counsel, handling any needs that might arise from the day-to-day responsibilities of running a business.

For her entertainment clients, Morris-Andrews drafts and reviews contracts including licensing, agent and artist agreements, and will negotiate deals on her client's behalf. Ranging from an independent play writer to a talent management company, Morris-Andrews assists her clients in whatever their legal needs might be.

CHAPTER 6:
WHAT TO CONSIDER WHEN PURCHASING HOME INSURANCE

By Gwendolyn G. Shaw
Financial Representative/Agency Owner
COUNTRY Financial

Homeowners have many factors to consider after purchasing a home. What kind of improvements will be made in the future? What work needs to be done immediately? And most importantly, how can the home and its contents be adequately protected?

First-time homeowners and experienced homeowners who wish to upgrade their current insurance policy should consider the following options when purchasing homeowners insurance.

First, consider the causes of loss to insure against. There are several types of coverages to choose from, but the two most frequently purchased are broad form and risk of direct physical loss coverage.

The broad form coverage provides protection for perils that are specifically listed in the policy declarations. Examples of such perils include fire, lightning, windstorm, hail, vandalism, and theft.

The risk of direct physical loss coverage is more comprehensive than the broad form coverage. In addition to the perils named above, it also covers accidental losses such as paint spills, ice damage, and counter-top burns. However, there are exclusions to this type of policy. Examples of losses excluded from the risk of direct physical loss coverage include earth movement, certain types of water damage, and intentional losses.

Secondly, homeowners should decide the level of coverage to purchase. Additional replacement cost is an option available on qualifying homes. If you qualify for this coverage and your home is destroyed, we will rebuild your home, even if rebuilding it costs more than the amount of insurance you have purchased.

The COUNTRY Financial group is among only a handful of insurers offering additional replacement cost coverage with no caps for qualified homes. That means COUNTRY will pay the costs (less, your policy deductible) to rebuild your house to the way it was should it be destroyed even if the cost is higher than your policy limit. With a no-cap replacement cost policy, you can maintain the financial security of your family even through tough times.

Homeowners might also consider purchasing replacement cost coverage for their personal property, such as televisions, DVD players, stereos, and computers. Replacement cost coverage allows for the replacement of personal property without depreciation.

A third consideration for homeowners is the deductible for their insurance policies. Higher deductibles result in lower premiums.

When deciding upon a deductible, homeowners should consider their ability to pay the out of pocket expense at the time of the loss. The minimum deductible suggested for homeowners is $500. However, homeowners should also consider increasing their deductible to $1,000 to reduce their premiums.

A fourth area of consideration is the amount of liability coverage to purchase. Liability coverage provides protection if someone is injured on your property, or you are responsible for damages to someone else's property. A minimum of a $300,000 limit is recommended to protect your assets. However, coverage can go as high as $1 million.

Buying homeowners insurance is a very important step in maintaining a household. Different homes warrant different policy coverages. With the help of an insurance representative, finding the appropriate policy coverages does not have to be a difficult decision.

Contact a COUNTRY financial representative for help determining the right coverage for your needs.

[1] Additional replacement cost is capped at 125 percent of the dwelling amount of insurance for Alabama, Georgia and Tennessee homeowners.
[2] Some special limits might still apply.

CHAPTER 7:
THE FENG SHUI OF BUYING A HOME

By Veronica Montinola

Buying a home is one of the biggest investments we can make. Housing costs are usually the largest expense in our monthly budget. This is true whether we rent or own.

For most of us, the decision to buy a home is based on emotion. This decision can sometimes change our life in ways we are not expecting.

Consider the possibilities in how Feng Shui can help you make a choice in one of your biggest investment. I know it will make a big difference in your life as it did for me.

With the help of some Feng Shui tips, you can take the experience of choosing a home to a higher level. Your home can be a great investment for health, family relationships, and wealth. Using Feng Shui can help you design a life that is more peaceful and harmonious.

Congratulations! If you are reading this book, it means that you are making a smart move. Being patient, learning how to choose the right house/unit can help you avoid a lot of unnecessary challenges, especially if you will be spending more than five years in this location.

There are three aspects to consider when choosing a home. In no particular order, they are:

1.What is the history of the Home?
To know who lived there and why they left are important. It indicates what energy is present in the home. Beware if a home is sold because there was divorce, bankruptcy, illness, or death.

2. What are the Exterior Features?
What do the roads look like? Are there water features nearby?

How is the neighborhood? What is the shape of the land? How are the neighboring buildings?

3. How does the interior feel?

Pay attention to your gut feelings the second you walk into the house or unit. You will know in the first few minutes whether this home is for you or not. Walk away if you feel uneasy.

Which aspect is the most important?

Out of the three aspects above, #2 is the most important. Because what surrounds your property, the exterior features, cannot be changed.

Aspects #1 and #3 can be changed and worked with if you are willing. So during your search, consider exterior features very carefully.

LOCATION, LOCATION, LOCATION

This is one of the basic and most important principles for Real Estate investment as well as Feng Shui.

A great location, great neighborhood, and good facing are a powerful combination. This is the type of combination that will shape our lives by influencing us daily without us realizing it.

-Great location. City or suburb? Which area within the suburb is the home/unit located? North area or south area? What are the features surrounding this house? Park, schools, ponds, shopping…water towers, electrical towers, cemeteries, hospital, churches…. You want to invest in an area where property values go up rather than down.

-Great neighborhood. Does it feel safe? Is it active and dynamic? What are the neighbors like? If you like a home or apartment, visit the area during the day, night, and weekends to get a better feel for the place. Taking time to do this is worth the effort. Once you move in, these are the things that cannot be changed.

- **Good facing.** What is the main door facing? Is the entrance clear? Is there something blocking it? Is there ample room for CHI or energy to gather? Is there any unsightly view nearby? Is it inviting?

It is also wise to look at the location of your bedroom, office, and kitchen. They are very important because these are places you will use often.

When looking for a home/unit, look around you with discerning eyes. Most often, the problem is outside the home and we are not used to looking for it.

Energy does not come from things inside the house; it comes from the outside environment. Things inside the home may make you feel good, but that is not where energy or CHI emanates from.

Avoid these negative features near you:

Sewage ponds, pylons, electric towers, communication towers, water towers, large antennas, unpleasant looking structures, and irregular or sharp edged buildings.

Look at highways, train tracks, airports, heavy traffic, and any rapid moving avenues that may emit negative energy.
Most often, these are features that are not included in a map.

So, take a drive around the neighborhood and avoid being within a mile of these features.

9 EXTERIOR NEGATIVE FEATURES TO AVOID

1. Roads. Cul-de-sacs are very popular in many neighborhoods. The circular CHI that gets distributed from the shape of the road outside the circle, affects all homes around it. Residents are more susceptible to suffer from negative experiences than in a home that has positive energy.

- T-shaped intersections create what is called "poison arrow." How impactful and damaging this energy is depends on how busy the street is, how long the leg of the "T" is and whether the road is on an incline. The "poison arrow" affects not only the home that is perpendicular to the leg of the "T," but also the homes that are directly next to it and across from the leg of the "T." Imagine water falling, when it hits the ground it splashes all around. Energy reacts the same way.

- Concave vs Convex refers to curving roads. This also applies to expressways that are above the ground and overpass sections next to buildings. You don't want to be on the outside of the curve receiving fast negative energy. It is best to be on the inside of the curve, protected from the cutting CHI energy.

- "U shape roads & y-roads. The "U" is similar to the cul-de-sac energy. Don't choose a building that is inside the triangle of a "Y" road.

- Dead Ends. Having a home or a building at the end of the road can bring in energy that is too strong. It is similar to the house at the tip of the "T" intersection

2. Water Features. If you bought a house near the water, it is best to have a balanced view. Have trees, shores, some land as well as other homes rather than just water.

- Best locations for water features such as pools, ponds, creeks, streams, lakes, and rivers is in the North, East, Southeast, Southwest.

Avoid them in the South and Northwest.

3. Train tracks. Having a train track behind your home is not conducive to a stable environment.

- In the city, some tracks are located around buildings. Choose units that are higher than the tracks to avoid cutting CHI.

4. Sloped terrain. Avoid homes with a sloped back yard. This means lack of support.

Example: Our neighbors built a beautiful 5,000 sq. ft. brick home.

A year later, the husband lost his job and was unable to find a comparable one. Their home was on the market for a while. They sold the home way below their price.

Price negotiation was not smooth. Their move was challenging.

5. Houses on top of the hill are completely exposed and have no protection from the elements. If the Wind is too strong, this means that energy escapes and cannot be contained. There is no benefit to those who occupy the space, life becomes challenging.

The same principle applies to a unit in a tall building, especially if there is an open view from front and back of the unit.

6. Shape of land. The best shapes are square or rectangular. A 1 to 1.6 ratio is best.

Avoid lots that are too narrow. If the lot is angled like a pint glass, it is best to have the entrance on the narrow side. A wider back indicates good accumulation of CHI.

7. Corner homes. Having one side exposed to traffic can influence the nature of work for those living in it. A busy road on the right side has the male traveling for work or gone often. The left side applies to females.

8. Who is taller? Avoid houses or buildings that are dwarfed by their neighbors on both sides. This configuration compresses the CHI making it difficult to grow.

Example: A client's business was on a slow decline after a couple of tall buildings were built next to them.

9. Other Miscellaneous tips:

- Be aware that hospitals are a place for sickness and death, they emit Y in CHI. It is important to practice good Feng Shui in this case.
- Same principle applies for graveyards and slaughterhouses.
- Homes below the street level need a lot of positive CHI.
- Multilevel homes need to be closely monitored.

Have a uniform theme throughout since the half levels are not whole. They are fractured levels of energy. - Homes and units around Police stations and Fire stations are not conducive to peaceful environments.

BEST FEATURES FOR A HAPPY HOME

• **Choose a vibrant neighborhood.** They are full of good energy. A good sign to see are lots of activities: people, children, pets, and well groomed yards. Avoid areas that are too quiet with vacant housing.

• **Choose a home with a good size front lawn.** This is called the "Bright Hall." It is the ability to accumulate "good CHI." Homes/units with their door too close to the street do not enjoy the best quality of CHI.

• **Have good landscaping.** It's a fact that good landscaping increases curb appeal and the value of the home/unit surroundings.

• **Observe this optimum formations for "water" placement:**
North, East, Southeast, Southwest
"Water": applies to pools, ponds, creeks, stream, lake, and rivers. Avoid the South and Northwest water locations. Water in the South douses fire element - hurts reputation as well as dampens opportunities for the eldest daughter. Water in the Northwest weakens opportunities for the man of the house.

• **Observe this optimum formations for "mountain" location:**
Northwest, West, Northeast, South
"Mountain" applies to hills, mountains, and higher grounds.

• **Which side should be higher?**
It is best to have the left side higher than the right. This principle applies to landscaping also. Higher trees or buildings are preferred on the left side. See the concept of Celestial Animals on the following page.

THE CONCEPT OF CELESTIAL ANIMALS

This concept is deeply rooted in Feng Shui.
The four celestial animals are: - Black Tortoise behind
- Red Phoenix in front
- Green Dragon at the left and - White Tiger at the right

This is the best formation to have. This formation has been observed for thousands of years. Many dynasties have risen and fallen due to this formation.

If you live in a building, the same thing applies. Taller buildings behind you become the supportive turtle.

Notice how the left side is taller than the right side.

A good dragon embrace is very auspicious. This can be achieved through landscaping. Small trees and shrubs.

For more on the Celestial Animals, follow this link for more information:

http://www.lspfengshui.com/single-post/2014/09/08/The-Four-Celestial-Guardians

• Good health and relationships are the basis of a good life. Building upon them is the science and art of Feng Shui. Being ill, stressed, and unhappy are not basis for creating a long and happy life.

MY STORY

As a young first time home buyer, I've been guilty of focusing my attention on the interior of the house. The truth is that energy comes from the outside, not the inside. It is the quality of the energy outside that comes in through the front door and windows that makes a difference.

Our first home was my best Feng Shui teacher. Looking back with Feng Shui eyes, it had a lot of negative features that led to the demise of my marriage.

- One of the negative exterior features was a big expressway about 100 feet in from the entrance, behind a neighbor's yard.
- The second, the house did not face our good directions.

See the resource page of my website for information.

- The house sat on a long and narrow lot.

- The house was located on a dead end street, the neighborhood was not vibrant.

I'll share some challenges with interior features, explained in the following chapter. One of the most important items are beds.

- Our bed was placed in the wrong direction.

- I had a wall of closet mirrors that reflected the bed. Eventually, a friendly third party came in between our marriage.

- Our kids broke their bones many times because of their bed placement.

- The front door was aligned with the back door, energy left the house as quickly as it came in. It gave us very little benefit.

- The home was a multilevel home that did not favor male energy, the North West.

- My then husband lost his business and was unable to get anything else off the ground. Depression, substance dependency, and ugliness set in.

- Luckily, the house benefited the female area, the

Southwest. I had a great job that allowed me to maintain and keep the house. My children benefited from it and so did I. It was a therapeutic transition.

- Unfortunately, the next buyers suffered a similar fate. After I received my Feng Shui training, I offered my free help. At the time, their marriage had already suffered, but they were still together. However, they decided to seek others forms of counseling instead. Their fate was forever changed when the husband took his life.

This example is one of the reasons I am passionate about Feng Shui. My mission is to help others understand that by making simple changes they can improve their life.

10 TIPS FOR HEALTHY INTERIORS

1) The Entrance is the mouth of CHI. It is where energy and vitality enters.

- Main Door should be clearly seen. There should not be two different entrances at front. This creates confusion.

- A front door should not be hidden by overgrown landscape. The front area should be easy to spot, bright and inviting.

- The front door should not be aligned with the back door. Otherwise energy leaves quickly and residents do not benefit.

• Apartment Entrances: Watch out for nearby columns, elevators, a fire escape, or garbage chute that may be directly aligned to your front door. If so, choose a different unit.

• Avoid long and narrow hallways, they produce sharp CHI.

2) The View:

Observe the view from the balcony, bedroom window, and kitchen window. Be sure there are no irregular shapes and forms directed to you.

3) Shape of the home - Best shapes are square or rectangular. As close to the sacred geometry ratio of 1:6. Energies are not evenly distributed when homes are too narrow.

4) Stairs and Hallways are like the veins and circulation of the home.

Avoid stairs that are too close to the door. CHI can rush in and out too quickly.

Avoid spiral stairs, they act as a corkscrew.

5) Fire features: This applies to fireplaces and location of the stove.

- Avoid them in the Northwest. They weaken male energy. Making it difficult for the male of the home to find progress and opportunities.

- Avoid fire features in the Southeast.

Example: Our friends enjoyed an upper middle class income. This is considered the 10% of the US. They had a modest home and two children. They had a fireplace in the Southeast. Having fire in the Southeast meant that money burned as fast as it came in. It was difficult for them to save money. They lived paycheck to paycheck.

6) Bedroom. The basic rule is to place the bed diagonally to the door. So you can see the door. Your feet should never align to the door or a window.

7) Bathrooms are best tucked away and not seen from the

main door.

8) Office. Similar to the bed, the desk should be placed diagonally facing the door. It should not be facing the wall. My client experienced a 15% increase in sales by using this placement.

9) Other miscellaneous tips:

- Avoid irregular or pointy houses and rooms, they create sharp corners and bad energy. They in turn can create havoc on relationships.
- Be sure you have plenty of light coming in. The lack of windows and light creates stagnant energy.
- Observe common sense; keep your home clean and clear. Keep your home free of humidity dampness. Bring laughter and music within. Love your home.

10) There is no perfect home unless you build it. The search may be challenging. There may be times when we'll need to compromise.

It is useful to make a list and prioritize. Remember to look for good exterior features and a house/unit with good bones. The rest can be worked with.

BEYOND THE BASICS

Every home has a natal chart. The natal chart is based on the direction and the period of the home. When life may not be going as expected, it is important to consult with a Classically trained Feng Shui practitioner. This along with observing the change in yearly energies can make life better and more enjoyable.

We live surrounded by energy. Everything around us is in a state of vibration and movement, even if it is not visible to us. The element of time is observed every year when a new animal sign emerges. This is the Chinese New Year.

Practicing the change of energy and updating your surroundings helps to stay in the positive flow of energies. Avoiding the negative energies is a great way to live a harmonious and balanced life. It is worth avoiding the bad energies that can set you back.

I feel grateful to be able to receive and share this information with you. It is information that was only shared with a privileged few in the past.

My intention is that you can put these tips into practice and allow you to live the life you deserve.

Happy home hunting!

MEET THE CONTRIBUTOR

Veronica was born and raised in Santa Cruz, Bolivia. Her wonderful parents agreed to send me to college in the US. After college, she worked as a Project Manager for Exhibits, Museums and Displays for 12 years. She always had an interest in Feng Shui and energy work. After the birth of her youngest son in 2005, she realized this was her calling.

Veronica became a certified Feng Shui consultant in 2011. In 2014, she became a Master Feng Shui consultant. To further enhance her practice, she is traveling to Malaysia in May 2017 to finalize her training in Chinese Astrology.

It is her great honor to help others using Feng Shui, Chinese Astrology and Chinese Metaphysical methods to better their health, relationships and opportunities. It is through working with the energies of the environment as well as the aspect of time that we can achieve balance and harmony.

When we live in the "Flow of Energy" life becomes simpler and better!

Veronica Montinola, Master Feng Shui Consultant
www.lspfengshui.com
www.facebook.com/LSP.fengshui
630-918-6954

CHAPTER 8:
HOW TO AVOID THE 5 PITFALLS OF WEALTH & BECOME FINANCIALLY FREE

By Jonathan Bautista

INTRODUCTION

Accumulating assets during your lifetime is extremely important, we are here to save our money, invest it, protect it, and be able to be financially free. What we have to avoid or watch out for are these five pitfalls so that you don't fall into trap of watching your next egg drained. This section is designed for you to understand the five pitfalls of wealth and what you can do to avoid them so that you keep all the hard earned cash and assets that you accumulate during your lifetime.

You know it is possible to not know what you don't know. It is possible to find out that all the things you've been doing to save for you future, plan for you future investments of your company, plan for the future financial independence and retirement of your career and ignition business, and planning for your children's college education. If you thought you were doing something right and later found it was wrong when would you want to know?

Before I got started in financial services, I grew up in a middle class neighborhood and was raised by a middle class family. My parents immigrated from the Philippines and they did the best they could. You know they did the best they could to raise us up in a philosophy of going to school, getting good grades, so therefore a company can take care of you and you're in the club. With that, with a piece of paper you're in the club, with that degree or that education. You're part of the inner circle. And for the most part that's what was taught for them. I was working for everybody else in my early years. I was working for everybody else, but my money wasn't working for me. All right? Robert Kiyosaki says that middle class people work for money. Rich people, wealthy people have money work for them. They understand their finances. Not only do they run the business, but they run their personal finances also like a business. But sometimes, in the case of business owners, the lines are blurred between business income and personal income, business checking account, and a personal checking account. Sometimes a business checking account turns into a cookie jar. And it shouldn't operate that way.

And I realized that being broke, the definition of being broke is a temporary situation. Creating wealth well that's a decision. Creating wealth that's a legacy. Creating wealth is creating systems that will allow you to predictably make money, and save money.

For over nine years, I've sought out some of the smartest, wisest, and wealthiest people, mentors and coaches who have the best wisdom to get people through tough times. Not just through the good times, but get people through the bad times, get people through when the winds of life come blowing by. These five pitfalls are principles which are a result of my constant and never ending improvement. These five pitfalls of wealth allowed many of these entrepreneurs and wealthy individuals to get ahead.

PITFALL OF WEALTH #1: LOSSES

Do you know anyone who has lost money 401(k)/IRAs? Or in real estate?

We're all hard workers, employees or business owners, we all work for a living, we earn money so wouldn't it make sense that we keep most of it, try not to lose it. So part of the five pitfalls is talking about that. So one of the things we do when helping families out is, we help them avoid losses.

Losses are Huge. Loss of a job, losses in investing in real estate, and every one of you have no doubt may have experienced the burn of losing money in the stock market. The banks, 401(k)s, real estate, these are some of the main vehicles people save or invest their money. Unfortunately, none of these can guarantee that you're not going to lose money...you don't have to go too far .... 2007, the market crashed, real estate bubble burst, 2008 and 2009 people lost 40 to 60% of their savings...people close to retirement, now they can't because they lost so much money. The average American 401(k) account experienced a 47% loss from 2005 to 2009.

The other place is the bank...People think banks are secure and safe, but they're actually not.

For example, if you have $100,000 and lose 10% then gain 10%, at the end of those two years you aren't even where you started. To say nothing about how long it takes you to recover (if you EVER can) if you sustain the kind of losses I listed above...just the kind of losses seen in the actual stock market in the past few years.

When Warren Buffet created his investment company back in the 1950-1960s and made his first decision to invest and be an investor, his first two rules he said was, "Rule No. 1: never lose money; rule No.2: don't forget rule No. 1."

Many families and small business owners, one of their greatest assets, was their home, was their real estate, whether it be residential or commercial real estate. I have an accounting friend who had a firm of four people, him and his partner, and two associates, his firm was very successful. Back in 2005-2006 they bought a commercial building. Had some good tenants in this commercial building. And within the commercial building they were running their own business as well. Well, just like a majority of the people during the crisis of 2008-2009 they're still dealing with it. Their $1.2 million commercial building is now $600,000 and guess what they owe? They owe $800,000. They're underwater. Well that's like many other people out there in America today.

The number one thing you want to avoid, especially if you own property, is that you have to understand, in 2006, according to the *Reuters Report;* U.S. baby boomers are house rich and retirement poor. Remember this is 2006. This is the height of the real estate economy. This is the height of the market. This is the height of everything going right. And even then people are retiring poor because the biggest asset they had was their property. How do you protect your greatest asset which is either your commercial real estate or your residential real estate? But people's situation was house rich, retirement poor, or real estate rich, house poor. What happened in the years coming? Well everybody became house poor, real estate poor, and retirement isn't even in question, because everybody spent their retirement money to try to keep the real estate afloat.

Now if you're retiring, if you're in 60s and 65, 70, 75, 80, somewhere in there you don't want to have the opportunity for you to un-retire. Because the losses, you ran out of money. Nothing that you did wrong. Right? Now that's the crazy thing about the losses, the real estate debacle, the mortgage crisis, 401(k)s, losing money. For most people they're doing everything right. You guys are running your business or household. You guys are paying your mortgage. You're paying your vendors or bills. You're paying your employees. You're doing everything right. But when this thing implodes what happened? It wasn't your fault. But what you can take control of, right? The White House and Washington they're going to do what they're going to do. It's our responsibility to do what's best for ourselves and what's best for our clients today. Unfortunately, unless you have an electoral vote, unless you are in the circles of politics, you don't really have a huge say so in the direction of our country. You do have a say so in your world, and avoiding loss is one of them.

PITFALL OF WEALTH #2: HEALTHCARE

Are you prepared to pay for unexpected medical expenses?

The 2nd pitfall of wealth is Healthcare and is one of the biggest causes of bankruptcy. You must be prepared for this trap and protect your savings now and in retirement. Current statistics reveal that by the age of 70, 1 out of every 2 people in America will need some sort of long- term care.

The number two pitfall is healthcare. You may be thinking when I retire I'm going to live on less money than when I was, expecting to live on when I was working because I have less responsibilities. Here's the reality. What I find is that many retirees, 60, 65, 70, 75, many of them now are spending more time not necessarily in their business. They're spending more time at the hospital. They're spending more time with their doctor. They're spending more of their time in pain. Alright? Recovering from something, and when you spend that much time recovering something, and seeing a doctor, that's not a free experience. That's something you have to pay your insurance for and if it's over your deductibles, you haven't met your co-pay yet you have to pay those things out of your own pocket. Here's the reality, 70% of people over 65 will require some form of long-term care services at some point in their life. Think about that. Half the people with a condition requiring help with health and personal care were under the age of 65. Furthermore, the average stay in a long-term care facility is 2 1/2 years at an average cost of $5,000 per month. That's an average expenditure of $150,000-$200,000 just for long-term care expenses...not to mention other medical expenses that might also be involved. If you go to government websites, it's about $2,000 to $6,000 for long-term care. Now what is long-term care? Long-term care is pretty much those 15 to 30 minutes when you wake up, Bathing, Dressing, Transferring, Toileting, Continence, and Eating. What's interesting is we have clients who works for a long-term care facility and they tell us these are not the numbers. If we want our family members or parents to stay in a mediocre facility then that's what you'll pay, if you want a good facility $10k or more, all the more reason to prepare for this pitfall. Families do not realize this until it directly affects them. If families don't have this in savings, they're going to use whatever it takes to pay for these facilities, whatever may be in their bank, savings, and 401(k). Families are then left with zero dollars because they exhausted their savings, their retirement savings, and they have to start from scratch, we don't want them to do that. We want them to be protected because eventually 1 in 2 will go through long-term care so we want to not only protect the individuals but also the family members so they don't go through these situations.

If you don't have a way to address these possible costs, most retirement savings will be devastated...and that's just if ONE person has significant health care needs...what if both husband AND wife had issues? This pitfall can blow a HUGE and deadly hole in your retirement savings.

PITFALL OF WEALTH #3: TAXATION

As if losses and unexpected medical expenses weren't enough…

You probably don't realize that Uncle Sam has his hand in your wallet...to the tune as much as 39.6%. Where do you think income taxes are going to go in this country in the future? Lower, the same, or higher?

Along with stock market losses, taxes take the biggest bite out of your finances. When you consider the tax rates of 15, 25, 35, 39.6% you can see that between Uncle Sam and state taxing authorities, almost 50% of every dollar you THINK you have actually goes to someone else than you!

Do you love to pay taxes? There are three places where you can actually save your money, and there are tax consequences when it comes to that.

You have to remember Illinois in itself just doubled the state income taxes a few years ago. Right? We're at the lowest income, federal income tax rate literally in the history of our country. We're at the lowest interest rate for borrowing money from the banks. Right? From the Federal Reserve, we're at the lowest interest rate. Where do you think these indicators are going to go in the future? And even though there's no guarantee that taxes are going to rise or they're going to the same or even go lower. A lot of people would bet the income taxes because of the war on terror, because of $17 trillion+ of a national deficit, because of cities filing bankruptcy. That people figure and they reckon that taxes are going to increase over time. Let's take a look at some of the problems that have been identified. Most people today don't fear death. What they do fear, 61% of people fear is living out of money. A lot of people run out of money in the future because they never accounted for paying taxes as they are today in the future. The impact of taxes, you have three basic buckets in which to place your money. Tax now on the left side, tax later or tax deferred in the middle, and the right side is tax advantage or in some conversations it could be tax free or tax never.

The first bucket is, TAX NOW. TAX NOW is Banks, Mutual Funds, CDs, or maybe Stocks. The money you save in these accounts, whatever interest you earn, you have to pay taxes. For banks I know if you earn $10 in interest, they'll send you a 1099 and when you do your taxes, you have to report it as income and you get taxed on it. It doesn't sound fair because it's only 10 bucks. But if you're saving, your serious money to retire on or to send the kids to college to get a college education, or start a business, or you're saving for your financial independence, putting your money in a 1% bank account may not make sense because not only is it a low rate of return, but you also get taxed on it.

The second bucket is TAX DEFERRED, or TAX LATER – this is your 401(k), IRA, Annuity...this money, the money you save now, you won't get taxed as it's growing, it's building and building up, but when you get to retirement age, or close to it 59 ½ and you start withdrawing money, you're going to have to pay taxes, if you withdraw before 59 ½, you get hit with a penalty of 10%. What happens when you defer something? What it is, we deal with it later on. Like many of these students who got a student loan. They're able to get a loan to get through their freshman, sophomore, junior year, and eventually graduate. But eventually, what happened? Their student loans were deferred and when they graduated within six months of them graduating, what do they have to pay? They have to pay their college loan back. And that's why when they don't have a job; they go back to school to get a Master's degree, hopefully to be more qualified to get a job. And what happens to their student loan debt? They add some more on top of their student loan debt. In the mean time, their student loan debt is deferred. But eventually you've got to deal with it when they graduate. Same situation here. We have to deal with taxes eventually when we contribute our money in 401(k)s, IRAs, annuity savings bonds.

The third bucket is tax advantage, or tax free. In other words, money that accumulates tax free could be accessed tax free. Roth IRAs are great for saving money, but the challenge is that you're limited to saving $5,500 per year. If you're over 50 years old, you can, and this year you can put $6,500 per year. The second option that you have to save in a tax advantage category is, an insurance based retirement plan. Commonly known, commonly known as an IBRP.

A majority of people know about banks and 401(k)s and these two vehicles fall into the first two buckets of tax now and tax later, where they are getting taxed. Why aren't people educated or informed about this column where you don't have to pay taxes?

PITFALL OF WEALTH #4: INFLATION

The next one is inflation. If people are saving their money in the banks because of fear, what they're going to face is that inflation down the road is going to erode their money. It's going to wear away the purchasing power of that dollar, for example, in 1973 in order for my dollar to buy the same things that a dollar did back in 1973. The average house back then was $32,500. The average house today is $159,000. The average car cost was $3,600 back then. Today it's $17,000. The average wage back then was somebody bringing home $7,500. Today it's $37,000. So consider where our future's going to go. If you're retiring today, you have a good chance of living another 15, 20, 25, 30 years. You've got to make sure that your money lasts just as long as you do. So therefore if you sell your company one day, you want to make sure that you avoid, at least, the four pitfalls. Number one, avoid losses, number two, avoid money being spent out for healthcare, number three, avoid that money being taken away from taxation from Uncle Sam, and cousin Illinois or whatever state that you decide to retire in.

What do you think banks give you as far as interest rate? Let's be nice and say 1%... let's take a look at what the government says inflation is. Inflation or the cost of living is 3%. If we did general math...what's 1 minus 3. It's a negative 2 percent. This is what people don't realize that if they keep all the money in the bank... let's say it's $100. That $100, if you look at your account without withdrawing your money, you'll have it there in a month, you'll have it there in a year if you didn't withdraw money which is good. That same $100, 5 or 10 years from now will not get you the same thing and that's what people don't realize that if they're losing money and they don't see it physically, that's what hurts them in the end. You have to make your money grow, because if you don't, you're losing money and you don't want to do that.

What will food, housing, gas cost 5,10,15,20 years from now??? Prepare now or be wiped out later. The risk here is that life expectancies are rising...as is the risk of outliving your money as the costs of EVERYTHING increases. Everyone has seen or had nightmares about being elderly and having to choose between food and medicine. What do you think basics like food, housing, medicine will cost, 5, 10, 15, 20 years from now? Not only must your money increase over time and adjust for inflation...it must also last as long as you do. Most retiree's greatest fear is outliving their money...is it your greatest fear? A proper retirement income plan in my opinion MUST contain the following components: provide guaranteed monthly income free from stock market losses and volatility, the ability for your money to last as long as you do, the ability to increase to adjust for inflation, the ability to create a monthly guaranteed income, and recover all you started with, generate a tax free income stream, and if you choose… to create a TAX FREE legacy to pass on to your heirs.

Remember, without proper planning, time is your greatest enemy and can devastate your retirement planning. With the proper planning, time can be your greatest friend.

PITFALL OF WEALTH #5: PROCRASTINATION

While there's certainly a cost of doing something....there's an even bigger cost of doing nothing! For better or worse, procrastination appears to be a part of human nature. Part of the heart of procrastination is fear...fear of making a mistake. In fact, that kind of fear is hard wired into our evolutionary make up. Procrastination affects everybody in different ways. Here we're talking about finances, but it affects families in relationships, if husband/wife don't talk about issues, procrastination builds up divorce, it also hurts people when it comes to health if they don't eat the right stuff, go to the doctor, you can't eat this. What if they would have taken care of their health from the beginning, it would've helped them out. In the case of finances, families I meet with say let's meet tomorrow or I'll take care of it tomorrow...there are seven days in a week Sunday, Monday, Tuesday, Wednesday, Thursday, Friday, Saturday ... tomorrow is not any of the days of the week that we have. I talk to families and this is what I say, if this stuff is important to them, let's pick a day where we can get back together and talk about this stuff. However, in almost all cases financial, WAITING ALMOST ALWAYS MAKES THINGS WORSE....NOT BETTER!! Don't pay your taxes because you don't have the money...you procrastinate and you pay the tax PLUS penalties. Get divorced but fail to review your beneficiary designations...you end of giving your ex-spouse $1,000,000 life insurance payment. Procrastinate around creating a proper retirement plan and not only you, but your family life suffers, your business suffers.

BONUS PITFALL OF WEALTH: LIFE INSURANCE

An extremely important discussion is on the evolution of life insurance. What are two things that are certain in this country? Yes, death and taxes! So why don't families have life insurance? Life insurance has evolved to the fact that people thought historically speaking, traditionally speaking that the only way to get benefits from your life insurance policy is one way, and what's that one way? If they died. It's usually people who have a term insurance benefit and the only benefit they get is, they don't even get it. It's the beneficiary that receives it. And what percent of people who never get the death benefit from term life insurance policy or a traditional life insurance is when they pass away.

But over the years the evolution or the upgrade of insurance has also happened. Kind of like the evolution of a business or the evolution of smartphones or the evolution of your Samsung and iPhones and right there's new models that come out with. Well the same thing happens when the richest, when of the richest insurers in the world which is these, the financial industry and more specifically in this conversation the insurance industry.

Next, in the 2000s that all changed. So people started receiving living benefits. People are receiving these insurance based retirement plan contracts to save for retirement. That it would supplement their 401(k). It would supplement the pension and it would supplement their social security. Because when they receive money from an insurance contract structured the right way, according to the IRS code 7702, now they're able to take money out from this policy without paying a dime in tax.

Now of course as retirement is not about your age, but how much you save. What if you could supplement your retirement income with something that grows tax deferred and that you can withdraw tax free? Well that's what insurance based retirement plans can do.

And then the insurance industry continues to evolve because they realized that many people are spending more money on healthcare.

So they included this terminal and critical illness component to these insurance contracts. Now I'm not saying that every insurance company has done this either. Unfortunately, there's (without me naming names) I can say that some of the giants of the industry have not upgraded their traditional policies. I don't know why. But if you face a terminal or critical illness, you face a heart attack, stroke, cancer. Alright? And your doctor says your life expectancy has been reduced because you face some health challenge, you can get an advance on your death benefit while you're alive. Let's say you had a million dollar policy, that could potentially mean that you'd get an advance of $250,000, $300,000, $400,000 while you're alive. You face terminal illness or some critical illness. What would you do if you knew you were terminal or you knew that your life was short? Or you faced for a heart attack, stroke, or cancer and then the health insurance paid for the procedures and the rehabilitations of, of your, of your situation. A life insurance policy today will pay you a benefit to help you, help you hire somebody of you caliber to run the position of the caliber. For therefore when you're back up, run back to 100% and you have less financial stress in the mean time. Be able to say, "Hey thank you for filling in while I was gone and we've got options for you at the company or not."

And the last one here (all the way on the right) is that life insurance today pays for long-term care. I got a client in 2000, 2001. She purchased a standalone long-term care policy just in case she needed some form of nursing home assistance or she needed to have the nurse come to her home. It's called home health care. Well she got a letter from her insurance company. They wrote her a letter stating that the conditions that in which they issued the policy have now changed and they offered her to keep her policy. They're going to increase her premium by 75%. She's paid into this policy for 10 years. Now they're going to increase it in order for her to keep her policy by 75%? So, today when you have a long-term care provision on your life insurance policy it doesn't have that wacky scenario. So you have a loan, so in other words you can take your $1 million death benefit policy, upgrade it to a modern contract, have long-term care and critical illness is a component of it. If you ever need long-term care you've got the money for it. Well there's your million dollar policy. If you needed care, I'm just throwing out a number, for 50 months, you can possibly have $9,900 a month to pay for your long-term care. And you are free to spend it however you want to spend it. You don't have to wait for an insurance company to say, "Well send us receipts and then we'll find out what we want to reimburse you and get you a check." Now life insurance today, if you have the right policy and you need long-term, care they will advance you a portion of your death benefit while alive for about 50 months. Every month for 50 months to help you get through your situation, maintain your financial dignity, help you pay your bills, help you pay for the expensive medical care cost without tapping into your business, without tapping into your home equity, without tapping into your brokerage account. That's the benefit of life insurance.

CONCLUSION

My hope is that you take some form of action to talk to the person that you trust or can trust to talk about the five pitfalls of wealth and completing your financial wall with life insurance to make sure that you're planning for your financial future. Get it done! It's not the strongest of the species that survives, nor the most intelligent. It's the one that can change. It's the one that can adapt. It's the one that can modify where they're going right now and still move forward without hoping that the world is going to be normal all over again. Focus more on retaining and keeping more of the wealth you create for yourself and for others. Keep more of your hard earned money and build wealth and build assets and build generational wealth. Have your money work harder for you rather than you working hard for the money!

MEET THE CONTRIBUTOR

Jonathan Bautista is an entrepreneur coach and financial coach with the goal of redefining his clients' future by giving them the information, tools, and guidance they need to take charge of their finances and create a better life. His crusade is to proactively educate the community in financial strategies, helping people identify hidden assets, and encourage them to turn missed opportunities into second chances.

He graduated with an accounting degree back in 2003 because during his freshman orientation in college, his professor told him that accounting is the language of business. The language of business meant a safe job coming out of college. He also wanted to own his own business one day, he thought if he knew the language of business this would be a good foundation. Four years out of college, he hated the 9 to 5 routine, sitting at his cubicle, and got sick and tired of counting other people's money. He then went into real estate investing… the years were 2007 and 2008. Not the greatest time to start investing in real estate, let alone start his entrepreneurial venture. And in 2010, he started a company alongside his sweetheart called Kids Wealth International Club teaching kids about financial literacy and about the rules of the money game. This wasn't enough, and the parents needed to be educated, and this is when he co-founded World of Wealth Group to educate parents on the rules of the money game. He's helped thousands of families all over America learn how to better save their money, invest their money, protect their money, and become financially free.

ABOUT THE AUTHOR

Wendy has been a licensed realtor in the State of Illinois for the last 15 years with large and boutique real estate brokerages over her career. She and her growing team of agents are strategically positioned across the Chicagoland area covering the state of Illinois from the Indiana border to the Wisconsin borders. She also has connections with a network of out-of- state realtors who are also able to assist anyone across the country with their real estate needs.

Wendy's vast experience in all areas of the marketplace including first-time buyers, resale, investment properties, short sales, and leasing affords her an in-depth knowledge base to pull from and advise you to make the best decision for you.

She listens to your needs, wants, and concerns and then leaps into action.

Wendy clarifies the home buying process and can put you in touch with any service you might need: including but not limited to selecting a lender, finding an inspector, an attorney, a contractor, or even a painter!

She is detailed in her work and customizes your home search. You won't receive a file with hundreds of listings that don't fit your exact needs. Wendy meticulously goes through listings and chooses the best fits for you based on your criteria and wish list in conjunction with her market expertise.

Whether you are selling new construction, a development, or a resale home, Wendy is able to help you get the highest possible price the market will bear.

She builds her business on dedication and personal attention to your listing.

She consults with you to prepare your house for sale and believes it's important a REALTOR® always shows your home.

Wendy is committed to being the resource on your home for potential buyers and highlighting its best attributes during customized tours. She understands the importance of marketing your home aggressively and will stay in active communication so you are always up-to-date on the sale of your home.

Wendy and her team are completely dedicated to YOUR REAL ESTATE NEEDS.